# CliffsNotes™

# The Age of Innocence

## By Susan Van Kirk

## IN THIS BOOK

- ■ Probe the Life and Background of the Author

- ■ Preview the novel in the Introduction to the Novel

- ■ Examine in-depth Character Analyses

- ■ Explore the significance of the work with Critical Essays

- ■ Reinforce what you learn with CliffsNotes Review

- ■ Find additional information to further your study in CliffsNotes Resource Center and online at www.cliffs.com

WILEY

Wiley Publishing, Inc.

*About the Author*
Susan Van Kirk holds a B.A. from Knox College and an M.Ed. from University of Illinois. She retired from English teaching at Monmouth High School and now teaches at Monmouth College in Monmouth, Illinois.

*Publisher's Acknowledgments*

*Editorial*
Project Editor: Suzanne Snyder
Acquisitions Editor: Gregory W. Tubach
Copy Editor: Katie Robinson
Glossary Editors: The editors and staff at Webster's New World Dictionaries

*Composition*
Indexer: TECHBOOKS Production Services
Proofreader: TECHBOOKS Production Services
Wiley Publishing, Inc. Composition Services

**CliffsNotes™ The Age of Innocence**

Published by:
**Wiley Publishing, Inc.**
909 Third Avenue
New York, NY 10022
www.wiley.com

# Table of Contents

# How to Use This Book

CliffsNotes Wharton's *The Age of Innocence* supplements the original work, giving you background information about the author, an introduction to the novel, a graphical character map, critical commentaries, expanded glossaries, and a comprehensive index. CliffsNotes Review tests your comprehension of the original text and reinforces learning with questions and answers, practice projects, and more. For further information on Edith Wharton and *The Age of Innocence*, check out the CliffsNotes Resource Center.

CliffsNotes provides the following icons to highlight essential elements of particular interest:

Reveals the underlying themes in the work.

Helps you to more easily relate to or discover the depth of a character.

Uncovers elements such as setting, atmosphere, mystery, passion, violence, irony, symbolism, tragedy, foreshadowing, and satire.

Enables you to appreciate the nuances of words and phrases.

## Don't Miss Our Web Site

Discover classic literature as well as modern-day treasures by visiting the Cliffs-Notes Web site at www.cliffs.com. You can obtain a quick download of a CliffsNotes title, purchase a title in print form, browse our catalog, or view online samples.

You'll also find interactive tools that are fun and informative, links to interesting Web sites, tips, articles, and additional resources to help you. See you at www.cliffs.com!

# LIFE AND BACKGROUND OF THE AUTHOR

# Formative Years

Born into a wealthy, aristocratic family, Edith Wharton grew up among the kind of people she wrote about in *The Age of Innocence*. After marrying, she divided her time between America and Europe, spending more and more of her time abroad. Her later years were spent in the company of fellow writers and she was recognized as the grande dame of American letters.

Born in New York City on January 24, 1862, Edith Newbold Jones was the daughter of George Frederic and Lucretia Rhinelander Jones. Her parents, descendants of Dutch and English colonists, were socially prominent with wealth from real estate, shipping, and banking. Edith's mother did not encourage her daughter's writing. Later, Edith saw her mother as cold and concerned with appearances; she saw her rarely in later life. Edith also had two much older brothers, Henry (b. 1850) and Frederic (b. 1846). Their lives were filled with servants, carriages, and social etiquette. From these happy childhood memories, the sensitive and intelligent Edith drew many ideas for her later writings about life among the leisure class.

Having suffered financial reverses, the family traveled through Spain, Italy, France, and Germany from 1866 to 1872 where the cost of living was lower. Edith learned German, Italian, and French before she was 10. In 1872, they returned to the United States, living on West 23rd Street in New York City with summers in Newport, Rhode Island. Edith was disappointed with America, finding New York City an ugly brown, and the architecture and interior decoration unsightly. She did not go to school but instead read from her father's extensive library and was taught by governesses. In 1878, Wharton wrote a book of poetry, *Verses,* that was printed privately. The editor of *The Atlantic Monthly,* William Dean Howells, put one of her poems in his magazine that same year. Her early writing was generally about the poor and their imagined harsh lives. By the time Edith made her social debut in 1879, she had written many early pieces. In 1880, the family went back to Europe and her father died at Cannes in 1882.

# Marriage and Depression

By 1883, Edith was 21 years old. In Bar Harbor she met Walter Berry, a Harvard graduate and lawyer who shared her literary interests and much of her life. She credits him with helping her writing style, and in later years she burned their personal correspondence. Biographers allude to this relationship as hopeful on her part, yet Berry did not propose to her.

She reluctantly married Edward Robbins ("Teddy") Wharton in 1885. He was from a similar social background, a Boston banker 12 years her senior who graduated from Harvard in 1873. He did not, however, share Edith's literary or artistic interests. During this time, she observed the new rich—the Vanderbilts and Astors—garnering details for her later works about life among the wealthy. She and Teddy bought a home called Land's End in Newport, lived in an apartment on Park Avenue in New York City, and traveled abroad. Throughout their marriage they would have no children. In fact, Edith went into marriage totally unprepared for the sexual side of being a wife; she did not find a passion that fulfilled her until much later in life. In 1894, she suffered the first of several nervous breakdowns, which biographers connect with her conflict between her social position and her writing ambitions. The unhappiness of her marriage was also a possible cause. Travel helped her depression and months in France and Italy not only gave her writing ideas, but also encouraged her love of Europe, a lifelong passion. In 1896, with architect and friend, Ogden Codman, she published her first book-length work, *The Decoration of Houses,* which encouraged a change from heavily decorated Victorian homes to simple classic designs that emphasized balance, symmetry, and proportion. By this time, she also had written more poems that were printed in *Scribner's* magazine, as well as a short story collection called *The Greater Inclination.*

## Passions, Artistic Friends, and Travel

During the first two years of 1900, the Whartons built a summer home in Lenox, Massachusetts, naming it "The Mount." Edith was an avid gardener and her home had extensive gardens. The novelist Henry James (1843–1916) became a lifelong friend during this time. Also from a wealthy family, James had traveled extensively, living in Paris and England, and shared Edith's sense of irony and humor. Theodore Roosevelt, whose second wife was a distant cousin of Edith's, met the Whartons when he visited Newport. Later, Edith attended the awarding of TR's honorary degree from Williams College; he dined at the Wharton's home on Long Island, Sagamore Hill, and he makes a fictional appearance in *The Age of Innocence.* During these years, Edith wrote her first novel, *The Valley of Decision.* In 1903, she toured Italy for material for magazine articles, and she also published another novella, *Sanctuary.*

A trip through England with Henry James in 1904 was the first of many motor trips through Europe that became part of Edith's life. She bought a Paris apartment in Faubourg Saint-Germain. Then she discovered her husband was keeping a mistress in Boston and misappropriating her money. She visited England without Teddy and began an affair with a journalist from the *London Times* named Morton Fullerton. He became the great love of her life and she found the passion that was missing in her marriage. In these years she wrote *Italian Villas and Their Gardens* and *The Descent of Man.* She also published one of her more famous novels, *The House of Mirth,* a social satire about Lily Bart, a beautiful but poor woman trying to marry rich to survive in materialistic New York City.

During this period, Edith socialized with such literary figures as James, Henry Adams, Bourget, Gide, and Cocteau as well as expatriate artists and writers. Teddy Roosevelt dined at her Paris apartment, she began a friendship with Bernard Berenson, and she published another short story collection called *Tales of Men and Ghosts.* By now, her husband, Teddy, had embezzled over $50,000 from her trust funds; he made restitution later by selling The Mount. By 1910, she was back in Paris and Teddy was in a sanitarium suffering from depression. His father had endured depression and committed suicide in 1891. Teddy would follow in his father's footsteps, having difficulties with depression until his death in 1928. Between 1910 and 1913, Wharton published *Ethan Frome, The Reef,* and *The Custom of the Country.* Continuing her friendship with Berry and Berenson, she legally separated from Teddy, later divorcing him in 1913. She spent the rest of her life in France.

## The War and Later Years

In 1914, Wharton urged America to join the war and carried on numerous efforts to help those in need. She founded the American Hostels for Refugees and the Children of Flanders Rescue Committee. Engaging in fund raising and visiting military hospitals, she also helped refugees coming into Paris after the battles of Marne and Ypres, finding them shelter, jobs, and food. She wrote *The Book of the Homeless,* asking for contributions from writers and artists, and giving the proceeds for war relief. For all these charitable deeds, she was decorated by the French Legion of Honor. In 1918, Wharton bought Villa Jean-Marie near Paris, naming it Pavillon Colombe. She divided her later years between this home and a chateau in the south of France, which was near Hyeres and named Chateau Sainte-Claire. Novels that came out of her war experiences include *The Marne* (1918), *French Ways and Their Meaning* (1919), and *Sons at the Front* (1923). The middle book was an attempt to explain French attitudes to Americans, as she had seen Americans come to Paris after the war and their actions were distasteful to her. As time went by, this abhorrence of American excess was replaced by a feeling that even the narrow-minded social code of 1870s New Yorkers had something noble about its ability to pass on civilized values. Meanwhile, she was becoming famous as an American woman of letters and she was awarded several prizes during these years. In 1920, *The Age of Innocence* was published, winning the Pulitzer Prize for Literature in 1921. Two years later, Wharton came to America for the last time to receive an honorary doctorate from Yale. In 1924, she was awarded the Gold Medal by the National Institute of Arts and letters, the first woman so honored. Over the next five years, she published several important works, including *The Writing of Fiction* in 1925, which discussed many contemporary writers' works and also elaborated on her own methods of writing. *The Age of Innocence* was adapted for the stage and opened at the Empire Theatre in New York on November 27, playing 207 performances. Also during this time, her friend Walter Berry and her ex-husband, Teddy, died. From 1920 to 1933, Wharton spent a great deal of time among authors and artistic circles in Paris. She published her autobiography, *A Backward Glance,* in 1934, which described the pleasures of her childhood, her early years as an author, and her friends and travels. In 1935, she suffered a slight stroke, but the following year she was writing again and published *The World Over.* In 1937, while visiting Ogden Codman's chateau, she suffered another stroke and died on August 11. She was buried in Cimitiere des Gonards in Versailles near Walter Berry. Posthumously, her novel *The Buccaneers* was published, completed by Marion Mainwaring. Wharton had begun it in 1934, and it was similar in theme to *The Custom of the Country,* concerning nouveau riche New Yorkers whose daughters go to Europe to seek out aristocratic European titles.

# INTRODUCTION TO THE NOVEL

# Introduction to the Novel

Between the late summer of 1919 and March of 1920 when Edith Wharton wrote *The Age of Innocence,* she was in her late 50s and highly sought after by publishers. Having lived through World War I in Europe and seen its tremendous destruction, Wharton turned readers' thoughts back to the time following the Civil War, when America's expansion, increased industrialism, and wealth from the railroads produced a group of robber barons and financiers, such as the Vanderbilts, Astors, and other newly rich families, who built huge mansions in New York City and began summering in Newport with the Old Rich. At first New York society rejected these "upstarts," but eventually the *nouveau riches* (New Rich) bent their talents toward social reform and philanthropy, which moved them up in the social order. They also began to marry their way into the Old Rich's circle, creating the interrelated families described later in Wharton's novel. *The Age of Innocence* shows the conflict brought about by this transition, with a main theme being the "right people" following the "correct rules" and marrying into the "acceptable families." Her characters, interiors, clothing, manners, settings, and attitudes reflect the world of her childhood and young-adult life among the Old Rich.

Over the years the interpretation and critical reception of *The Age of Innocence* has changed, keeping step with the attitudes of the times. When the novel first came out, the reading public supported Newland's decision to go through with his marriage to May. May's lie about her pregnancy to Ellen—so that she could save her marriage—was either overlooked or considered the appropriate thing to do. Ellen, "the other woman," was afforded no sympathy. In 1921, when *The Age of Innocence* was awarded the Pulitzer Prize, beating out Sinclair Lewis' *Main Street,* the committee declared that *The Age of Innocence* "best present[ed] the wholesome atmosphere of American life and the highest standard of American manners and manhood." Even Wharton was taken aback when reviewers failed to see the irony of the title and her social criticism of 1870s New York society.

Currently, Wharton's book is admired as a "modern" novel. More sympathy is extended to Ellen as an independent woman, and more criticism is leveled at May's manipulative ways. Feminists cheer Ellen's independence and values, but also criticize Wharton's role as a member of the group she is criticizing. The varying interpretations but consistent approval of the love-story triangle have made *The Age of Innocence* a timeless classic. The Scorsese film of the novel in the early 1990s only heightened its popularity.

Despite these interpretations of the characters' motives, Wharton had great difficulty in deciding what to do with her unhappy lovers. At one point she decided to have Newland and Ellen run away together, but have Newland eventually go home because he could not give up his leisure-class values. Another option had Newland and Ellen spending a short time in Florida; Newland becoming unhappy with living a lie and Ellen eventually returning to Europe. Wharton also considered Newland and Ellen marrying, but Ellen later forsaking him for Europe with its less narrow-minded attitudes. In the end Wharton decided to keep them apart and use their love to show how individuals must sacrifice happiness for duty and the greater good of the social order. The patient, time-honored values of the old century have given way to the expediencies of the new one, and the reader closes the book judging the gains and the losses.

## Brief Synopsis

It is a January evening in 1870s New York City and the fashionable are attending the opera. As young Newland Archer, lawyer and man about town, gazes up at his soon-to-be fiancée, May Welland, in the Mingott-family opera box, he is disconcerted by the arrival of May's cousin, the Countess Ellen Olenska, who has left her profligate but wealthy Polish husband. To discourage gossip, Newland decides to announce his and May's engagement at the Beaufort's ball that night.

All of old New York is at the ball, gossiping about the Countess. Later, when the family plans a dinner to introduce her to society, no one accepts. Without delay, the Mingott family enlists the help of ancient social sages, Henry and Louisa van der Luyden, to shore up support by inviting old New York to a dinner it cannot refuse. In this way they introduce the exotic Countess, and she finds New York society charmingly narrow and provincial compared to Paris. The next day Newland visits the Countess's small house in a Bohemian section of town. He finds her drawing room exotic and her friendship with shady financier Julius Beaufort unsettling. But he senses her loneliness and, despite some misgivings, sends her yellow roses.

The Mingotts enlist Newland's boss, Mr. Letterblair, to ask Newland to dissuade the Countess from seeking a divorce. When Newland speaks with Ellen—a passionate and exotic woman, unlike his quiet, innocent May—he finds himself falling in love with her, despite his engagement. Worried by temptation, Newland flees to Florida where

May's family is vacationing and asks May to move the wedding date up. Startled, May tells him that if there is "someone else," he may have his freedom. Touched by her selflessness, Newland returns to New York. As he confesses his love to Ellen, a telegram arrives from May, saying that they can be married in a month. Newland knows his duty.

Book II of *The Age of Innocence* begins with May marrying Newland as New York society watches. By August, a year later, Newland and May have settled into a fashionable if boring life in New York, living in a wealthy part of town and spending summers with the rest of the rich in Newport. Ellen has moved to Washington D.C.; she returns to stay with her grandmother briefly, but later leaves to visit Boston. Still under her spell, Newland lies to his wife and follows Ellen there. Ellen promises to stay in America only if they do not hurt May with a clandestine affair. She returns to Washington. Meanwhile, Julius Beaufort's shady financial dealings catch up with him, and his wife, Regina, appeals to Ellen's grandmother for help. Mrs. Mingott suffers a stroke and sends for Ellen to nurse her; during the two-hour carriage ride with Ellen from the train station, Newland suggests they have an affair. Ellen refuses, knowing that will hurt May. He abruptly leaves the carriage and walks home. Seeing May in the library, he realizes he will dutifully stay married to her forever.

Undaunted, the next day Newland meets Ellen at the Metropolitan Museum, where she finally agrees to a future one-time affair. Elated but guilty, Newland decides to confess all to May, but she interrupts to tell him that Ellen is leaving for Europe and the Archers will give a farewell dinner for her. Shocked, Newland intends to later follow Ellen. At the dinner, however, he suddenly realizes that the entire family, including May, thinks that he and Ellen are already having an affair; giving Ellen the funds to live in Europe is the family's way of dealing with the situation. That night as he and May retire, she announces that she thought she was pregnant and told Ellen earlier, before she was really sure. But now she is sure, sealing Newland's fate forever.

The years pass. Newland is 57 and he and May have two grown children: Dallas and Mary. May has recently died of pneumonia, nursing a third child to health. Newland accompanies Dallas to Paris on a business trip, where Dallas tells Newland the Countess Ellen Olenska has invited them to dine. Newland has not seen her in 26 years. Dallas confides to his father May's deathbed confession that Newland sacrificed the one thing he loved because of duty and honor. That evening outside the Countess's apartment, Newland encourages Dallas to go up without him. In Newland's memory, their love stays forever young, perfect and unchanging over time.

## List of Characters

**Newland Archer**   A young New York lawyer who marries May Welland. Throughout the novel he struggles between integrity and individual freedom, eventually choosing a life and marriage of narrow conventions. He falls in love with the Countess Ellen Olenska, only to sacrifice that passion for a life of duty.

**May Welland Archer**   A young socialite, who marries Newland and settles down to a totally conventional life, following the lead of her mother in all areas and representing the societal attitudes of the wealthy social class and time period.

**Countess Ellen Olenska**   A granddaughter of Catherine Mingott and a cousin to May, she returns to New York society from a life in Europe, married to a dissolute but wealthy count. Causing a stir in New York society by her unconventionality, she symbolizes a life of freedom from social restraints.

**Mrs. Manson (Catherine) Mingott**   Grandmother to Ellen, Catherine Spicer Mingott is a wealthy widow equally at home in Europe and America. Although unconventional in some of her behavior and attitudes, and outrageously obese, she meticulously lives beyond reproach in her personal life.

**Henry and Louisa van der Luyden**   Gruesomely preserved symbols of old wealthy families that trace their ancestry to pre-Revolutionary America, and arbiters of social taste, the van der Luydens cause New York society to accept the Countess as long as she behaves. They have a country estate, Skuytercliff, and a house in the city where only a select few are invited. They are not opposed when they make their opinions known.

**Medora Manson**   Ellen's aunt, and guardian after Ellen's parents die. She unconventionally raised Ellen in Europe and America. Her eccentric behavior, multiple marriages, financial woes, and travel are tolerated by New York society because she was born into the wealthy class, and, despite her unusual behavior, she is one of "theirs."

**Mrs. Archer and Janey Archer**   Newland's mother and old-maid sister, respectively, who live together and are more and more identical as time goes by. They are devoted to Newland and love to gossip. Mrs. Archer is strongly opinionated, especially about social behavior, and Janey is a sheltered romantic; both viewpoints are indulged by their dinners with Sillerton Jackson, as they revel in his gossip about the wealthy.

**Lawrence Lefferts and Sillerton Jackson**   Two men who function as a Greek chorus, commenting on both good taste and the family histories of New Yorkers in the story. Lefferts is an outrageous womanizer, but New York forgives him because he is male and is from old wealth. Jackson is an oldmaidish gossiper who never misses a chance to pass on scandal and connect it to his 50-year backlog of New York families' histories.

**Julius and Regina Beaufort**   A couple whose marriage Old New York society condones because she is from an old wealthy family. His background of financial irregularities and his many adulterous relationships are ignored because he is rich and male. His ostentacious lifestyle and scandalous behavior add a bit of spice to the gossipers, and he pursues Ellen Olenska for much of the story.

**Ned Winsett**   Newland's friend and a failed journalist and critic, Winsett is a symbol of what happens when one leaves the straight-and-narrow, socially conventional life.

# Character Map

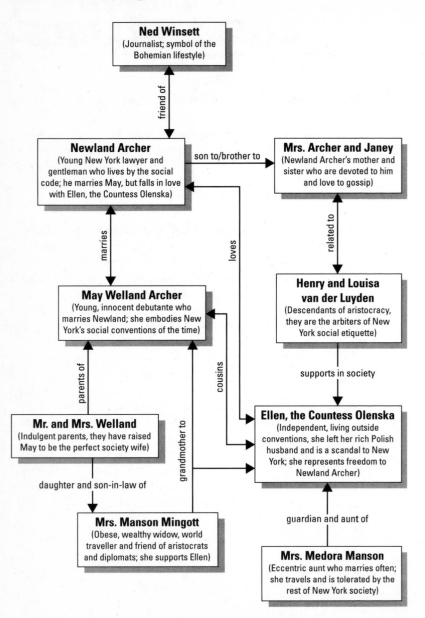

**Ned Winsett**
(Journalist; symbol of the Bohemian lifestyle)

*friend of*

**Newland Archer**
(Young New York lawyer and gentleman who lives by the social code; he marries May, but falls in love with Ellen, the Countess Olenska)

*son to/brother to*

**Mrs. Archer and Janey**
(Newland Archer's mother and sister who are devoted to him and love to gossip)

*marries*

*loves*

*related to*

**May Welland Archer**
(Young, innocent debutante who marries Newland; she embodies New York's social conventions of the time)

**Henry and Louisa van der Luyden**
(Descendants of aristocracy, they are the arbiters of New York social etiquette)

*parents of*

*cousins*

*supports in society*

**Mr. and Mrs. Welland**
(Indulgent parents, they have raised May to be the perfect society wife)

*grandmother to*

**Ellen, the Countess Olenska**
(Independent, living outside conventions, she left her rich Polish husband and is a scandal to New York; she represents freedom to Newland Archer)

*daughter and son-in-law of*

**Mrs. Manson Mingott**
(Obese, wealthy widow, world traveller and friend of aristocrats and diplomats; she supports Ellen)

*guardian and aunt of*

**Mrs. Medora Manson**
(Eccentric aunt who marries often; she travels and is tolerated by the rest of New York society)

# CRITICAL COMMENTARIES

## Book 1
# Chapter I

## Summary

It is a January evening in the early 1870s at New York City's fashionable Academy of Music—where the conservative, old rich families come to see and be seen. *Faust* is the opera and the theatregoers are watching the stage, but they are also observing the delicious dramas in the exclusive boxes of old New York's First Families.

Newland Archer, young lawyer and man about town, arrives stylishly late and, like his friends, observes the box of old Mrs. Manson Mingott where Newland's soon-to-be fiancée, May Welland, is sitting with family members. Newland considers with warmth and approval the virginal white of May's dress, gloves, and flowers. His mind leaps to the intimacies of the honeymoon and he thoughtfully considers his role as husband in initiating her into the sexual pleasures of married life.

Newland is sitting with two other gentlemen of New York society: Lawrence Lefferts and Sillerton Jackson. Lefferts is an expert on social etiquette, while Jackson is the acknowledged source of information on family connections, characteristics, and scandals. Both gentlemen are staring in amazement at the Mingott box where an unknown woman has just entered and seated herself near Newland's girlfriend. Her entrance causes Jackson to question the Mingott's decision to allow her presence here among the elite of New York society.

## Commentary

Wharton's first chapter sets the tone of irony and hypocrisy that delineates the fabric of her old New York, the 1870s setting of *The Age of Innocence*. In her first, richly detailed chapter, she introduces old New York's social order, its code of conduct and superficial values, and the main characters that will interact within its boundaries.

The reader begins to see a motif: New York society is composed of closely knit families that close ranks and follow behavior codes handed down from mother to daughter, father to son. Wharton opens her story in that cultural symbol of the Gilded Age, the Academy of Music. Wharton is very accurate in her knowledge of the building, the seating order, and the patrons' behavior. Because members of old New York society use the Academy of Music as a marriage market to reproduce their class and facilitate marriages within their ranks, they seat debutantes modestly near the rear of boxes. Married ladies sit near the front displaying valuable possessions—jewels. This way others can envy the husbands who provide the jewels, and the husbands can display the wives they possess. The carefully proscribed social seasons also are a way for the old rich to retain control because interlopers—the New Rich—are trying to break into their ranks (see "Introduction to the Novel").

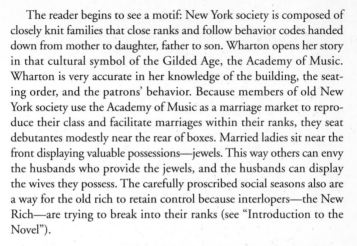

It is through Newland's eyes that we view the society of 1870s New York. Ironically, Newland sees himself as cosmopolitan, but Wharton belies this sentiment by describing his acceptance of "the German text of French operas sung by Swedish artists . . . [and] . . . translated into Italian for the clearer understanding of English-speaking audiences." This is Wharton's humor, but Newland sees this as perfectly understandable. He parts his hair "with two-silver-backed brushes with his monogram in blue" and he has a gardenia—the socially acceptable flower—in his buttonhole. Everything about Newland Archer screams conformity.

Edith Wharton exposes the society's double standard regarding marital beliefs. May, Newland's soon-to-be fiancée, is a virgin with no "past," dressed in white and carrying white lilies of the valley. In contrast, Newland takes pride in his own sexual experience gained in a previous two-year with a married ("safe") woman. May is the perfect society bride: Newland's role will be to train her in social tact, wit, and the art of "attracting masculine homage while playfully discouraging it." Ironically, Wharton mentions that if Newland dug down deeply enough in his vanity, he might realize that a sexually knowledgeable wife would be much more sophisticated and eager to please. Throughout the novel she undercuts Newland's opinions to expose the hypocrisy of the social code.

While Newland broadcasts "conventional," May Welland radiates "innocence." Sitting forward, her face slightly flushed, she watches the opera whose words she likely does not understand. Wharton purposely chose an opera based on a play by Goethe where the older, more experienced Faust falls in love with the young, beautiful village girl, Marguerite, whose innocence parallels that of May Welland. May does not understand Faust's efforts to seduce Marguerite, but her romantic innocence is underscored as she looks at Newland's flowers and blushes.

Watching all these actions are two minor characters, yet their presence throughout the book enforces Wharton's themes of societal hypocrisy. Lawrence Lefferts is one of the biggest hypocrites in the novel. While judging others who break the social code, he is later protected by the very code he breaks. Sillerton Jackson is a prudish, prim, and pretentious Victorian who excels at gossip and back stabbing. He, like Lefferts, uses his opera glasses to peruse the crowd and comment on their behavior. Throughout the novel these two will provide words and actions that propel the plot and sometimes cause mistaken assumptions in their social group.

## Glossary

(Here, and in the following chapters, difficult words and phrases, as well as allusions and historical references, are explained.)

**Above the Forties**   farther out from the fashionable center of the city.

**Mr. Luther Burbank's...prodigies**   students of Luther Burbank (1849–1926), an American plant breeder and horticulturist.

**chemisette**   a detachable shirt front formerly worn by women to fill in the neckline of a dress.

**Josephine look**   a gown in the style of the first French Empire (1804–1815) named after Napoleon's wife, Josephine, empress of France (1804–1809); with a short waist, decollette bodice, flowing skirt, and short, puffed sleeves.

# Book 1
# Chapters II–III

## Summary

Newland is feeling embarrassed because the males in the audience are watching the Mingott box and he is trying to decide on a course of action to protect his beloved May from scandal. He realizes that the mystery lady must be May's cousin, the Countess Ellen Olenska, who recently arrived from Europe. Disgracefully, she has left her husband and is staying with her grandmother, old Mrs. Mingott. While Newland approves of family loyalty in private, he would prefer the Wellands not exercise it in public with the "black sheep" of the family.

Newland listens to the other men make jokes about Ellen's past and his embarrassment grows. He waits for the curtain to signal the end of the act and does the loyal and manly thing: He dashes for the Mingott family box where May gratefully consents to his request that he announce their engagement. She then introduces him to her cousin, Ellen, who recounts tales of them playing together as children. Newland interprets her attitude toward New Yorkers as flippant and it irritates him.

After the third act, Mrs. Regina Beaufort leaves the opera house as a signal that her annual ball will begin in thirty minutes. Regina is from the South Carolina Dallas family, a "penniless beauty" who is not too bright, but her looks are stunning. Introduced to New York society by a cousin, Medora Manson, she married Julius Beaufort, who came with a doubtful past. He is known to enjoy the company of women other than his wife. Arriving at the Beaufort home, Newland describes their sumptuous rooms and possessions, but he is having second thoughts about family loyalty. May calms his unspoken fears by explaining that the Countess excused herself because her dress was not fashionable enough to attend such a party. Relieved by this information, Newland decides that May shares his viewpoint about dealing with this "unpleasantness;" what a perfect wife for any man to possess!

## Commentary

Character
Insight

Wharton increasingly pulls the reader into a world of conflicts and hypocrisy. The old New Yorkers are both drawn and repulsed by the money and possessions of the New Rich, as symbolized by Julius Beaufort's rise in social status. Though old Mrs. Mingott's English son-in-law sent letters of introduction with Beaufort, rumors circulate about his "dissipated habits" and cynicism. Speculation holds that he left an English banking house under questionable circumstances. His affairs with women and shady past are disregarded because he carries things off with style. The Old Rich tolerate the Beauforts because they have a ballroom that is used just for one night and closed off the other 364 days a year.

Theme

"Few things seem more awful to Newland than an offence against Taste." He finds Ellen's words distasteful as she humorously mentions that New York will be judging her. But that is exactly what his friends did in snickering about her past. Who knows what scandalous things she has been doing in Europe as a woman alone, and now she is here at the opera pretending to be a person of taste! Here the reader sees clearly the double standard of society and Newland's complicity: toleration for Julius Beaufort and contempt for Ellen Olenska.

## Glossary

**double entendre**   a term with two meanings, especially when one of them has a risqué or indecorous connotation.

**bouton d'or**   (Fr.) golden or lustrous buttons; here, part of the interior décor that causes lustre and glitter.

**aigrettes**   bunches of the long, white showy plumes of the egret, worn for ornament on a hat or in the hair.

# Book 1
# Chapters IV–VI

## Summary

The "precise and inflexible" engagement ritual begins. Newland, May, and her mother go to old Mrs. Mingott's house, where the pleasantries turn to the family blessing, the engagement ring, and the wedding day. During this conversation, Ellen and Julius Beaufort unexpectedly arrive. Ellen extends an impromptu invitation to Newland to come visit her; however, Newland privately thinks she shouldn't ask an engaged man to call on a married woman. The next evening, Mr. Sillerton Jackson dines at the Archer's and spreads gossipy information with his acerbic tongue. He criticizes Ellen for walking up Fifth Avenue during fashionable hours with Julius Beaufort, a married man. Totally out of character, Newland takes up Ellen's defense, saying that her bad marriage was a matter of poor luck. Later, in the study when the men are alone, Jackson reveals that Ellen was allegedly living with her husband's male secretary a year after her "escape," and Newland defends her again.

After Jackson leaves, Newland sits alone in his armchair before the fire considering his upcoming marriage and the disturbing influence Ellen's arrival has had on his thinking. How could he defend Ellen's deeds when religious and social standards see them as reprehensible? His worst fears are confirmed when the Lovell Mingotts send out invitations to a formal dinner for Ellen, and New York society rejects the invitation within 48 hours.

## Commentary

Visiting Mrs. Manson Mingott is intriguing. Her huge physical appearance is comedic and if she had not had such a scrupulous past, she would be a character from a wicked French novel. Her position allows her to make critical comments that others cannot make. Implying that Mrs. Lemuel Struther's arrival is like fresh meat, she personifies New York as a carnivorous creature needing new blood.

In these chapters, Newland begins a puzzling defense of Ellen. While Mrs. Archer questions what their ancestors would have thought of Ellen's behavior, she knows what current New Yorkers think. It is one thing to be ignorant of New York's social code, but another thing to be told and not comply. Newland appears to totally defend Ellen, and it is puzzling that somehow Newland is forgetting the double standard favoring men.

However, alone in his study, we see another side of Newland and his thoughts about women. His society disallows women knowledge about life outside their narrow existence; in fact, his sister Janey is a perfect example. His fiancée, May, is also totally naïve and Newland feels that husbands and wives must live in a world "where the real thing was never said or done or even thought, but only represented by a set of arbitrary signs." Before Ellen came, he had no problem with this code; why has her arrival had such an unsettling effect on him? Despite his protests to Jackson, "nice" women cannot be as free as men. But why should Lawrence Lefferts' marriage be the gold standard, where a man can have numerous affairs, but his wife must not do the same? Newland defends Ellen's right to be "free," but contemptuously calls the Count's women friends "harlots." Obviously, women who are "free" trouble New Yorkers.

## Glossary

**embonpoint**  plumpness; corpulence.

**Siren Isle**  (Gr. and Rom. mythology) home of any of several sea nymphs, represented as part bird and part woman, who lure sailors to their death on rocky coasts by seductive singing.

**heiroglyphic**  a picture or symbol representing a word, syllable, or sound; hard to interpret or understand.

**Chippendale**  designating or of an eighteenth-century English style of furniture characterized by graceful lines and, often, rococo ornamentation.

**Patroon**  a person who held a large estate with manorial rights under a grant from the Dutch government of New Netherland.

# Book 1
# Chapters VII–VIII

## Summary

The van der Luydens are one of three New York families with aristocratic bloodlines. They listen to Mrs. Archer's account of the slight conferred upon the Countess by New York society, and decide that a show of family loyalty would rectify the situation. Because Louisa's relative, the Duke of St. Austrey, is arriving from Russia, the van der Luydens will include the Countess in their dinner and reception for him.

At the party, the van der Luydens spare no pains in providing the best china, silver, and glassware. Newland notices that the Countess is pale but very confident with almost a regal bearing. She does not seem decadent, as her past would suggest. However, when Newland and the Countess speak after dinner he is shocked by her sadness and candor. She wants to be all things American and when she touches his knee with her fan he feels unexpected electricity. Breaking an unspoken social rule, the Countess says she will see Newland at five o'clock the next day. Surprised, he agrees. Later he watches couples—including the Lefferts, who initially turned down the Archers' invitation—standing in line to be introduced to the Countess now that the van der Luydens have included her in their social circle.

## Commentary

Wharton uses word painting to describe the intolerant, rigid older generation. The van der Luydens symbolize the frosty chill of old New York. Newland believes Louisa has been "gruesomely preserved in the airless atmosphere" like "bodies caught in glaciers keep for years a rosy life-in-death." Louisa defers to her husband almost sacredly and Newland has a disturbing vision of his own marriage in future years. The van der Luydens hold family loyalty as sacrosanct. Mrs. Mingott remarks, however, that New York society needs new blood. The van der Luydens are the proof.

Wharton personifies New York society as having eyes and ears because the van der Luyden's carriage in front of the Mingott household is instant news. As "arbiters of taste," the van der Luydens contrast considerably with Lawrence Lefferts. Newland says that Lefferts conspired to keep everyone away from the Countess's dinner because he had neglected his wife and he needed to point a hypocritical finger elsewhere to keep her from discovering his latest indiscretion. Mrs. Archer remarks, "It shows what Society has come to." While Lefferts is tolerated despite his known indiscretions, the Countess is ostracized until the family gives an outward appearance of accepting her.

**Literary Device**

Dinner is a wonderful venue for contrasting old, cosmopolitan Europe with upstart, provincial New York and Wharton wastes no time in ironically portraying their attitudes. One would expect the Countess and the Duke, as representatives of European royalty, to be concerned with the stuffy rules of society, but instead, they ignore the rules. The New Yorkers, products of the "new world," might be expected to be free and liberated, but instead, they are the ones commenting on breaches of etiquette.

## Glossary

**ormolu**   imitation gold leaf.

**Patience**   the British name for the card game Solitaire.

**"Esther . . . Ahasuerus"**   a biblical allusion that compares Mrs. van der Luyden's intercession with her husband to that of Esther, who interceded with Ahasuerus to save her people [Esther 7–9].

**Debrett**   biographical reference books chronicaling the British Peerage and Baronetage; a respected "Who's Who" of British meritocracy.

**Diana**   (Roman myth) the virgin goddess of the moon and hunting. Here, a symbol of May Welland's innocence and virgin purity.

# Book 1
# Chapters IX–XI

## Summary

Newland goes to Madame Olenska's small, rented house "far down West 23rd Street," in a strange, Bohemian quarter. The Countess is not home, so Newland has ample time to look around her drawing room. The room is intimate and exotic, unlike the staid, conservative rooms of his life. He realizes that his and May's future drawing room will be nothing like this; it will be traditional and conservative. Eventually the Countess Olenska arrives with Julius Beaufort who leaves her at her door. She is house hunting because her family will not let her stay where she is even though the street is respectable. Newland counters that it is not "fashionable." Madame Olenska's candor is expressed when she tells Newland, "why not make one's own fashion?" Throughout their conversation she states candid opinions and he is shocked by her frankness. He tries to warn her that New York society does not like honesty, and she should be listening to her female relatives for advice. He would like to warn her to refrain from driving with Beaufort, but he prudently keeps silent. The Countess wins his sympathy when, sobbing, she explains how lonely she is. During her distress Newland forgets formalities and calls her "Ellen" twice, and then guiltily remembers May. The Duke of Astrey and Mrs. Struthers arrive, and she invites Madame Olenska and Newland to her salon on Sunday. Madame Olenska agrees, but Newland is silent. Leaving, Newland stops at a florist shop to order May's daily lilies of the valley. Seeing richly hued, yellow roses, he considers sending them to May; but instead, without his card, he sends them to the Countess.

Newland's conflict continues. On a Sunday walk with May, he mentions sending roses to Ellen; May finds it odd that Ellen did not mention them. Again, he and May discuss the wedding date, and Newland is struck by May's lack of imagination or original thought. Their conversation leads him to regret the sameness of everything, including her expected reactions to his expected comments. The next afternoon Janey announces to Newland that Mrs. Archer is agitated because Madame Olenska has been seen at Mrs. Struthers' with the Duke and Julius Beaufort. In the midst of the argument, Henry van der Luyden arrives, explaining that he went to see the Countess Olenska to pass along some friendly advice. He says that the Duke does not realize "our little republican distinctions" and is leading Madame Olenska into mischief. Because the Duke was a guest in his house, van der Luyden feels he must explain the Duke's actions in an acceptable manner. Likewise, because Madame Olenska told Mr. van der Luyden that she would be grateful for his guidance, he has defended her to Sillerton Jackson.

Newland works at the legal firm of Letterblair, Lamson, and Low. His boss, Mr. Letterblair, asks him to represent the Mingott family in dissuading the Countess Olenska from seeking a divorce. He gives Newland two letters to peruse, one from a French legal firm about finances and the other from the Count. A deadly quiet dinner with Mr. Letterblair emphasizes scandals that have brought down families and Newland's boss states three points: the Mingott family is against divorce, the Countess does not want the Count's money, and it would be wise to avoid a scandal that could only hurt the Countess and the Mingotts. Newland reluctantly agrees to take the case, but refuses to solidify his stance on the divorce until he has spoken to Madame Olenska. He sends her a note and she agrees to talk to him.

## Commentary

**Literary Device**

Newland is experiencing a conflict of feeling: He is caught in a matrimonial snare, yet he has always adhered to society's rules. With more bridal calls to make from "one tribal doorstep to another," Newland perceives himself "shown off like a wild animal cunningly trapped." Should he have told May that he is calling on Madame Olenska? Should he be content with his in-laws' decision on the house he will occupy and with his wife's conventional interior decoration? Wharton highlights this conflict by placing him in Madame Olenska's drawing room, which is charmingly arranged with unconventional paintings. Even the smell of the artfully arranged flowers is exotic. This seems like freedom. Ellen contrasts her drawing room with the gloominess of the van der Luydens.' Why must everyone be exactly alike? Newland has not questioned that idea before.

Madame Olenska is totally destroying the balance in Newland's world, and, to make matters worse, she brings out his protective instincts. When she confesses to her loneliness, he suggests that New Yorkers have opened their arms to her. However, she candidly tells him something he realizes but does not want to accept: New Yorkers do not seem to want to hear "the truth" and she feels very lonely among people who request that she pretend. Her distress causes him to drop his formalities, improperly take her hand, call her by her first name (Ellen), and then guiltily remember his fiancée.

Newland is playing with fire. The vivid yellow roses are too strong for his insipid fiancée but perfect for the Countess Olenska's free spirit. He places his card with the roses for Madame Olenska, but—conscience stricken—withdraws it. Two boxes of flowers, one white and one golden, are going to two women. With one he would live an orthodox life; with the other he would be free. One seems to lack imagination and original thoughts—a person suitably symbolized by bland, white lilies-of-the-valley—while the other represents the passion and imagination of yellow roses.

**Literary Device**

Newland's conflict is far from over as evidenced during his conversation with May. His concern that she will stare "blankly at blankness" is certainly revealed by her inability to make any decisions herself. Even Newland's desire to travel is followed by May's thoughts of how she will explain this to her mother, who does not understand doing things "differently." When Newland tries to explain his new-found ideas about being free, she counters with the belief that his thought is "like people in novels . . . vulgar. . . ." Newland would like to think he could be unconventional, but May more truthfully realizes that they would both hate resisting social pressures.

First May reminds Newland that he is at heart a conventional person, and then his dinner with Mr. Letterblair adds emphasis to that idea. Through this somber dinner, Wharton reminds the reader that Newland works in an atmosphere of old line New York legal retainers. While he enters the room desiring to rebel against convention, Mr. Letterblair convinces him that a divorce will not be wise for anyone. While Newland reconsiders his thought that Ellen should divorce, he finally agrees to represent the Countess because his concern for her protection outweighs his sense of prudence as an engaged man. He makes numerous excuses for her past, thinking that women in Europe might be drawn into affairs from sheer loneliness. What the Count's letter to the Countess alleges is never revealed, but Newland's reaction suggests that in it the Count hints or states that she had scandal to hide in her past. Newland never questions the Count's statements and his decision is partly based on his desire to protect her and her "pitiful figure."

Theme

Newland's motive is also based on his own affair with Mrs. Thorley Rushworth. The double standard in sexual liaisons is foremost in Newland's mind. As his mother would say of men's affairs, "such things happened." It was "foolish of the man" but "always criminal of the woman." This double standard is passed down from aunts, mothers, and other female relatives. There are "women we love and respect" and so we marry them, and "women we enjoy and pity" with whom we have affairs. Newland's continuing conflict is between considering Ellen as a person who should be respected and free, or thinking of her as the woman with whom he desires an affair. At this point he decides he will speak with her and save her from the censure of New York society that would be brought on by a divorce for any reason.

## Glossary

**vitrines**   a glass-paneled cabinet or glass display case for art objects, curios, etc.

**in extremis**   (Lat.) at the point of death.

**labyrinth**   a complicated, perplexing arrangement, course of affairs, or the like.

**denouement**   outcome, resolution.

**lapis lazuli**   an azure-blue, opaque semiprecious stone; a mixture of various minerals.

**inanition**   emptiness; exhaustion; lack of strength or spirit.

**importunate**   troublesome; annoyingly persistent.

**clandestine**   kept secret or hidden, especially for some illicit purpose; surreptitious; furtive.

**sedulously**   persistently and steadily; diligently.

**Book 1**

# Chapters XII–XIII

## Summary

On the way to Countess Olenska's house, Newland sees Beaufort's carriage leaving for some dark assignation. He considers, as he walks, the many differences between his mother's world of the leisure class and the world occupied by artists and creative people. But when he reaches Countess Olenska's house, he finds Beaufort there. Angry, Newland feels once again like her protector. The Countess dismisses Beaufort, leaving Newland triumphant.

Newland tells Madame Olenska that he is there to discuss business with her. He stresses that New Yorkers have "old fashioned ideas," and while it might be legal to divorce, it is not accepted socially. Further, the Count might bring up scandalous accusations and, true or not, she will be ruined. Here he pauses, but the Countess is silent, leading Newland to believe there might be some truth in the Count's allegations. He explains that she is financially provided for and free, so why divorce simply to have what she already has? She asks if he agrees with the family and when he does, she decides to drop the divorce request.

Ten days later, Newland is in Wallack's theatre and he feels an unexplainable sadness after watching a sad scene of lovers parting in "The Shaughraun." May, in Florida with her family, has asked him to "be kind to Ellen." Ellen, too, is at the theatre. Newland joins her and the Countess asks him if the character in the play will send his lover yellow roses. Newland blushes; he is becoming entranced with Ellen Olenska as a person "to whom things were bound to happen."

## Commentary

**Literary Device**

Through Newland's thoughts, Wharton points out the huge differences between the social conduct of Europe and America. The writers, musicians, and artists who live in New York City's Bohemian quarter, while often odd or eccentric, are mainly respectable. Mrs. Archer, however, views them as disreputable and living in poverty.

Newland sees Madame Olenska's society in Europe as a place where creative people and scientific thinkers are welcome. While he is drawn to writers like Ned Winsett who seem to live in a world of exciting ideas, he is also reminded of the restrictions on his own life. Beaufort's friendship with the Countess Olenska also reflects the disparity between American and European values. When Newland goes to her home and finds Beaufort there, she is dressed in a red robe with black fur, which Newland considers a sensual and improper attire for a virtuous American lady. It is, however, the latest thing in Europe. While Beaufort and the Countess might be at home in Europe, Newland most assuredly would not be.

**Literary Device**

Divorce is discussed at length in the context of social values. Newland explains to the Countess that the collective interest of society outweighs the needs of the individual. In New York, people believe the institution of the family must be protected. Ellen Olenska will be sacrificed if she divorces. The irony of Newland's mission is revealed as his feelings for Ellen increase in spite of his belief that he must be loyal to the family. He, too, is an individual being sacrificed to society's collective interest: its desire to replicate itself by proper marriages between correct people.

## Glossary

**parvenu**  (French) nouveau riche; a person who has suddenly acquired wealth or power.

**dissimulation**  pretense; hypocrisy.

**imprevu**  [Fr.] unforeseen.

**milieu**  environment; esp., social or cultural setting.

**blackguard**  a person who uses abusive language; a scoundrel or villain.

**hackneyed**  made trite by overuse.

**histrionic**  overacted or overacting; theatrical; artificial; affected.

## Book 1
# Chapters XIV–XV

## Summary

As Newland leaves the theatre he meets Ned Winsett, an acquaintance and writer. Winsett is bitter about working for a women's weekly to support his family while he struggles as a writer. He suggests that Newland consider politics, where he can "get down in the muck" and accomplish good.

Newland is unhappy when this conversation ends because after he is married, these discussions will not occur. Three days later he receives a message from the Countess saying she is visiting the van der Luydens' country estate and wishes he were there also. He contacts the Reggie Chiverses, rescinding previous excuses to visit them and plans a country weekend near her.

Newland seeks the Countess at Skuytercliff, but she is out and he sets off to meet her. They go together to the privacy of the Patroon's house, another van der Luyden property. During their visit, Newland's reaction to Ellen is becoming clearly sexual: his heart beats rapidly and he imagines her putting her arms around his neck. Their reverie is broken by the arrival of Julius Beaufort. Newland is annoyed by Beaufort's undeniable pursuit of the Countess. The next day Newland is back in his office, his reverie in the country a fading dream.

Newland receives a note from the Countess asking to see him. Considering several possible replies, he gives up and flees for St. Augustine, where May is wintering with her parents.

## Commentary

Wharton emphasizes the totally separate worlds of the leisure class and the artisans through the conversation between Newland Archer and Ned Winsett. Newland has never been invited to Ned's home or met his family. Newland does not seem to realize that soap, cleanliness, and fashionable clothing cost precious money to those in the lower class. Ned must face realities totally unknown to Newland, such as putting food on the table and a roof over his family, and if that means writing for a women's weekly, that is what he must do. He suggests that Newland get into politics, saying that Newland's class is a leftover from Europe and will never cause social change until they "get down in the muck." While the rich worry about social change, they do not dirty their hands with politics. Newland tactfully sidesteps the subject, but continues to be unfulfilled by the "gentlemanly pursuit" of law, where he reads newspapers each day in his office.

**Literary Device**

The unthinkable is becoming a conflict in Newland's mind and Wharton takes the opportunity to pursue this struggle. She spins a scene of pure romance and escape by placing Newland and the Countess together in the Patroon's cottage. Newland first sees the Countess in a red cloak against the snowy landscape, and he is enchanted by her exotic difference from the society ladies he knows. She appears to expect him when she says, "Ah, you've come." For the first time, he imagines her embrace and his total attraction to her is evident. When Beaufort arrives, Newland measures his chances with the Countess against Beaufort's and considers what might attract her to Beaufort. Even when he is back in New York, Newland cannot focus on his beloved new books, except for a book of poetry that raises his passionate longing. In considering a future without Ellen, Newland realizes, he is suffocating in the future planned for him by his upbringing and his promises. His decision to flee to Florida and May causes the reader to question whether he is trying to fight his temptation for the Countess—a socially unthinkable attraction—or his decision to pursue his social duty and stay with May.

## Glossary

**bock**   a dark beer traditionally drunk in the early spring.

**epistolary style**   of or suitable to letters or letter writing. Here, the distinct manner of the Countess's letter writing.

**grand tour**   a tour of continental Europe, formerly taken by young men of the British aristocracy to complete their education.

**Book 1**
# Chapters XVI–XVII

## Summary

When Newland sees May in St. Augustine, he feels assured that their engagement is the right thing to do. He tries to think of an argument to persuade Mrs. Welland to agree to an earlier wedding date, but cannot. Nor can Newland persuade May, who fears that he has changed and innocently asks if he has "someone else" in his life. She says that Newland can end their engagement and she will understand. Newland is momentarily frightened, but then the veil of innocence again covers her eyes and he assures her there is no one else.

Returning home, Newland has dinner with his mother and sister Janey, and he learns that the Countess visited them while he was away. He calls on old Mrs. Mingott to intercede on his behalf over the wedding date. During their conversation Ellen arrives, and, as he leaves, Newland quietly makes a time to see her the following evening. When he arrives the next night, the Marchioness Manson, Ned Winsett, and a Dr. Agathon Carver are in the Countess's drawing room. Crimson roses are evidence of Beaufort's continuing pursuit. When the gentlemen leave, Mrs. Manson thanks Newland for his concern over Ellen and begs him to send Ellen back to the Count because she is giving up a huge fortune for an inferior social position.

## Commentary

**Character Insight**

Newland views May and her mother as totally innocent, unimaginative women who stubbornly stick to "stupid conventionalities." Behind Mrs. Welland's concern for the future of her daughter, however, is an iron will that he somehow misses. Mrs. Welland has no compassion or sympathy for Ellen's predicament, strongly disapproves of "foreigners," totally rejects any discussion or approval of divorce, and consistently rejects arguments to change the wedding date because it might violate the dictates of the season.

May is not as unimaginative as Newland thinks. Sensing something terribly wrong, she trammels on customary etiquette and speaks out about her fears. When she offers to sacrifice herself, Newland admires her generosity and selfless devotion to his happiness. No, nothing is wrong if they can push the wedding up before he is overcome by his growing attraction to the Countess. May has fought back in a way she knows will succeed: Newland is not going to defy convention and break off a well-advertised engagement to the perfect wife.

**Literary Device**

Wharton is approaching the end of her first book and must increase the pressure on Newland Archer to act. She does so in three cryptic conversations that take place in Chapter 17. The first conversation is with Newland, Janey, and Mrs. Archer. When Newland expresses surprise that the Countess called, Mrs. Archer looks down at her plate and Newland thinks she is annoyed at his surprise. Perhaps, however, she is hiding her concern over Newland's friendship with the Countess. She certainly hints at that by comparing Ellen to "her ideal"—May.

The second conversation occurs with old Mrs. Mingott, who playfully asks why he did not marry Ellen, and then mentions that it is too late now. Under her watchful eye, Newland and Ellen exchange messages that are, as always, in code. When he hears she is going out the following evening, he is annoyed that it is probably with Beaufort, again conveying his attraction.

The final conversation with Mrs. Manson reveals the irony of Newland's position. Mrs. Manson implores Newland to help Ellen have the best life. That life is married to the rich Count under their social rules. When Newland says he would rather see her in hell than back with the Count, Mrs. Manson asks him if he is being selfish and would an affair with a rich man be a better choice than being a rich, but legally married lady?

## Glossary

**polonaise**  an eighteenth-century dress with the skirt divided in front and worn looped back over an elaborate underskirt.

**French leave**  an unauthorized, unnoticed, or unceremonious departure; the act of leaving secretly or in haste.

# Book 1
# Chapter XVIII

## Summary

The Countess finally comes into the drawing room and, seeing the crimson roses, becomes angry and asks her maid to take them to Ned Winsett's wife, who is ill. Her aunt is also sent on to Mrs. Struthers' salon and, finally, Newland and Madame Olenska are alone.

He hurts the Countess's feelings by asserting that her aunt thinks she will go back to the Count. She cannot believe that Newland gives credence to this, and she turns the conversation to his wedding. Newland tells her that May thinks he wants to hurry the wedding in order to forget about someone he loves more. When Madame Olenska asks if he does indeed care more for someone else, he sidesteps the question, saying he will not marry anyone else. A long pause follows.

The carriage comes and the Countess should be leaving, but Newland takes her hand and says there is another woman that he would have been with if it had been possible. This angers Madame Olenska because he was the one who made it impossible by talking her out of a divorce. Her words make him realize that the "scandal" she worried about was not her own; she was worried about the scandal of divorce for the Mingott family.

Newland tells her that he loves her. She cries and he explains that they can still have each other because he is still free and she soon could be. Recklessly, he says he will not marry May. But Ellen Olenska, unable to hurt May, says, "I can't love you unless I give you up." Irrationally, Newland snaps that Beaufort will probably replace him. Nastasia, the maid, comes back with a telegram. It is for Ellen from May, who says that old Mrs. Mingott's arguments worked, and they will move the wedding to right after Easter.

When Newland arrives at his home, a second telegram is waiting and Janey has stayed up to find out what it says. He asks her the date of Easter and when she replies, he laughs ironically, and realizes he will be married in a month.

## Commentary

**Literary Device**

This amazing chapter states the novel's dilemma the strongest thus far. Wharton's expert use of irony shows that Newland's arguments about suffering, endurance, and denial—that social, religious, and class standards must be upheld or all is chaos—have not been lost on the Countess. She has learned from him that one cannot win one's freedom by sacrificing the happiness of others. She reminds him that his own selfish interests have to be sacrificed for the good of honor, family, and principles. Ironically, these were his very thoughts earlier in the novel.

**Theme**

In many ways, Ellen Olenska is an adult Edith Wharton, living a European life of intellect and the arts, outside the boundaries of New York society. Wharton came to realize in her own life that men such as Newland Archer do not understand women but need them to settle down and lead responsible lives. Men must support and protect women and not hurt them by having affairs or engaging in shady business ethics. (See "Life and Background of the Author.")

The ironic timing of May's telegram shows she has once again anticipated Newland's moves and robbed him of his chance. Despite thinking her dull and conventional, Newland does not realize how manipulative she is.

## Glossary

**ubiquitous**   present, or seeming to be present, everywhere at the same time; omnipresent.

**chignon**   a knot or coil of hair worn at the back of the neck.

**"Ah, don't make love to me!"**   in nineteenth-century attitudes, this remark of Ellen's means "do not flirt with me or pretend to pursue me romantically."

**inscrutably**   not easily understood; completely obscure or mysterious.

# Book 2
# Chapters XIX–XX

## Summary

Newland stands on the chancel step of Grace Church, waiting for his bride, his mind is utterly in a fog. When Medora Manson enters, Newland strains to see if Ellen has accompanied her, but Ellen has not come. Newland has to be reminded to give May his arm. The ceremony ends and all go to the wedding breakfast.

The couple changes after the wedding breakfast, enjoys the traditional rice shower, and goes to the train station where they will journey to a country estate near Skuytercliff. When they arrive, the van der Luyden's servant informs them that they will have to use the Patroon's house because of a water-tank leak. May is excited, but Newland is all the while thinking of his afternoon there last winter with Ellen.

The following autumn finds Newland and May in London, having spent three months touring on their honeymoon. They are invited to dinner with a Mrs. Carfry and her sister, acquaintances of Newland's mother and sister. May is very uncomfortable and has no interest in exchanging pleasantries with two non-Americans who are strangers. Once back at the hotel, Newland and May discuss the hostesses, their invalid nephew, a vicar and his wife, and a French tutor named M. Riviere. May dismisses the tutor as very "common looking," but Newland had enjoyed talking with him about Parisian literary figures.

## Commentary

Literary Device

Wharton overwhelmingly sets a tone of irony in this wedding where the groom loves someone else. Newland, trapped in this social institution, muddles through the dignified ritual as if it were unreal. He senses the death of his spirit and even imagines the onlookers in their correct pews when he eventually enters the afterlife. Seeing May, he realizes there is no turning back.

Wharton also reveals the values of this society. Newland has handled the obligatory duties of the groom. His choices would all be approved by Lawrence Lefferts' satisfactory comments on "Good Form." Newland thinks back to when those things were so important to him, and he realizes how meaningless they were. "And all the while, I suppose . . . real people were living somewhere, and real things happening to them."

**Literary Device**

Buried alive in tradition and New York form, he watches his chances of freedom fading. The ultimate irony is that he and May will spend their wedding night in the very house where Newland and Ellen sought a safe haven. Unaware of her irony, May excitedly explains "it's the only house [Ellen's] seen in America that she could imagine being perfectly happy in." Newland drops deeper into the void.

The forced intimacy of the three-month wedding tour reveals Archer's fears that there are things he does not like about his new wife. She does not like to travel, she pouts, and she reveals a snobbishness that gives her an icy exterior. Her world is New York City and she will "always be loyal, gallant and unresentful," but also unflinchingly provincial. In short, she is exactly what she has been trained to be: the perfect wife with no clue about her servitude. Newland enjoys and even envies the impoverished tutor because he has spoken with literary figures in Paris, but May speaks of him with disdain. While Archer copes by thinking the first six months of marriage are the most difficult, he also fears May is rounding off any tendency of his to be less than conventional. He begins to see his servitude as she arranges his orthodox life.

## Glossary

**alacrity** eager willingness or readiness, often manifested by quick, lively action.

**vicissitudes** difficulties that are likely to occur.

# Book 2
# Chapters XXI–XXIV

## Summary

It is August, a year later, and life has set into a predictable pattern. The Archers spent the winter in the new house and rode in the new brougham the Wellands purchased for them. Newland has arranged his library, met Winsett and young friends for drinks, and he and May have attended the opera. They are back in Newport—Newland rather reluctantly—and it is late summer.

It is the Newport Archery Club's annual tournament and May confidently wins. As he watches, Newland is struck by the change in Julius Beaufort's appearance; he has aged considerably and Wall Street rumors say he is in trouble because of speculation. After the tournament May suddenly suggests that they see Old Mrs. Mingott. She shows her grandmother the expensive brooch the Beauforts gave her for winning first place. Then Newland is sent to get Ellen who is visiting for the day. He finds her on a pier by the seashore and silently watches her. When she does not turn around, he walks back up the hill.

On the drive home May suggests Ellen has changed and might be happier if she returned to her husband. Newland is shocked and says May is being cruel. But later that night he lies awake, contrasting his dull life with a romantic vision of Ellen riding home in the moonlight.

When the Wellands receive an invitation to a party for Mrs. Blenker and her daughters, Newland surmises that Ellen might be in the area since Medora Manson is a friend of the Blenkers. While Mr. Welland and May take a drive and Mrs. Welland goes to the party, Newland takes the opportunity to look for a horse at a stud farm near the Blenker cottage. He finds himself longing for Ellen like an addiction. He speaks with one of the Blenker daughters and finds out Ellen has been called away with a telegram from Boston. She will be there two days and is staying at the Parker House. Sensing a chance to give his life a change from its "endless emptiness," Newland decides to pursue her to Boston.

The next morning Newland takes the Fall River train, telling May he has business in Boston and will go on to New York. Fortunately, a letter from his law firm arrived the night before, giving credence to his lie, and no one seems suspicious.

When in Boston he sends a message to Ellen at Parker House, but the messenger returns saying she is "out." Newland, surprised, walks to Parker House and sees her sitting on a bench in the Commons. She is startled to see him. Traveling unconventionally without a maid, she has met an emissary from her husband. The Count has offered her a huge sum of money if she will return and "sit at the head of his table occasionally." She refused but is to meet again with the emissary at 11 a.m. Instead, Newland suggests they take a steamboat ride to Point Arley and dine.

Sensing his idea of an "adventure," Ellen writes a note and they take a cab to Palmer House where she takes the note inside. Newland sees a familiar man that seems out of place in the crowd while he is impatiently waiting, but he cannot recall his name. They journey to the steamboat and ride to Point Arley in silence. It is a comfortable silence and Newland does not want to break the feeling of the moment. They find an inn for lunch and, because it is noisy, he asks for a private room. She puts his conscience at rest by making it seem natural because they are old friends.

At lunch Newland hears about her past 18 months and, while she appreciates New York taking her in, she cannot understand why it wants to be a carbon copy of Europe. When he asks why she does not go back to Europe, she confesses it is because of him. He has made her understand a sensitive and exquisite love in comparison to her life in Europe. When he admits that his marriage is a sham, she cries quietly because her life is empty also. Ellen promises to stay as long as she can see him, but they must not betray May. Though he does not want to believe that this is all they can have, she assures him that it is. He holds her for a moment and she promises not to go back to Europe yet.

## Commentary

A minor melody plays through these chapters as we see a glimpse of Julius Beaufort's fall from favor. His mysterious past was alluded to in various conversations and now Newland notices that he has aged considerably. Rumors about speculation, risky investments, and lack of caution surface. Still, he puts on a wonderful Archery Club Tournament each year; May received an expensive diamond-tipped arrow pin and "there was no denying that Beaufort did things handsomely." Interestingly enough, Beaufort is the only character that honestly comments on May's vague intellectual shortcomings and perhaps gives a glimpse of how others see her.

**Character Insight**

Right on the heels of May's snobbish comments about the French tutor in England, Wharton continues—during the Newport scenes— to show that May is firmly in charge of Newland's life. She is her mother's daughter. No longer the quiet mouse, she arranges every minute of Newland's days. The Wellands have purchased the home Newland will occupy and the brougham that transports him. When he expresses reluctance to go to Newport, it is his mother-in-law who says nonsense, and May must show off her Paris gowns. May's triumph at the picture-perfect Archery Club win and her calculated suggestion that they visit Ellen's grandmother are both symbols of how deeply Newland is entrenched in the leisure-class New York lifestyle. He is restless and the constraints of that life weigh on him, but his reluctance to fetch Ellen at the seashore shows that his dreams of life with Ellen are only fantasies. He would never give up his position.

**Theme**

Wharton creates doubts about all his restlessness when Newland describes May as "peace, stability, comradeship and the steadying sense of an inescapable duty." This is 1870s, nostalgic New York as Wharton sees it from the new century. Marriage is a steadying influence in a sea of chaos soon to be visited by World War I. The idea that Newland ever dreamed of marrying the Countess is described as a ghostly memory. Even Medora Manson reminds Newland that "marriage is one long sacrifice."

Even married, he is haunted by Ellen. He lies to May about his true intentions in going to the Blenker's, and then recklessly follows Ellen to Boston for a tryst aboard a tourist boat. "The longing was within him day and night, an incessant, undefinable craving, like the sudden whim of a sick man for food or drink once tested and long since forgotten." Unlike Newland, Ellen realizes they cannot exist outside the roles they have been groomed to play by society. Their love must be pure, or innocent people will be hurt. Newland reluctantly agrees.

**Character Insight**

Newland is still a man torn. When he is with May on their honeymoon, he reverts to the old patterns of male gratification and social norms. He feels comfortable in this pattern but is strangely restless. He does not realize—as the reader does—that May's iron will designs his monotonous days. His longing for a fantasy life is fulfilled by his thoughts of Ellen. He declares that his marriage is a sham and he agrees with Ellen that New York is "damnably dull . . . [with] no character, no color, no variety." At the same time Ellen realizes, with far more insight than Newland, that they are prisoners of their world. "There they were, close together and safe and shut in; yet so chained to their separate destinies that they might as well have been half the world apart."

## Glossary

**bedizened**   dressed in a cheap, showy way.

**duologues**   a conversation between two people.

**stylographic**   a fountain pen having a pierced, conical point (rather than a nib) through which the ink flows.

**Ida Lewis**   Idawalley Zorada Lewis [1842–1911]. The best known lighthouse keeper of her day, she tended the Lime Rock beacon on a tiny island a mile from Newport. Credited with saving 18 lives, she became famous for her unconventional life. It is not surprising that Wharton twice mentions Ida Lewis as Newland views the nontraditional Ellen from afar.

# Book 2
# Chapters XXV–XXVI

## Summary

Returning to New York City, Newland again sees the face he saw in Boston—this time recognizing him as M. Riviere, the tutor from London. They meet that afternoon and Riviere explains that he is Count Olenska's messenger. He tells Newland that the Count has sent new proposals to the Countess's family, and Newland realizes—in shock—that her family has purposely left him out of the discussions of these proposals. Remembering May's comments about Ellen at Newport, he realizes that his abrupt disagreement signaled to May that her family can no longer trust his opinions; therefore, they are now excluding him from the family council.

Although M. Riviere had discharged his duty to the Count honestly, he tells Newland that he earnestly feels the Countess should not go back to the Count and he hopes Newland will convince the family. Riviere has seen a change in Ellen and he attributes it to his belief that the moral standards in America are more pronounced than those of Europe. Ellen's family has been led to believe the Count misses her because that was the message he sent; however, Riviere says that is not the case and he hints that Ellen would be subjected to much unhappiness if she returned.

Soon it is November and four months have passed since Newland last saw Ellen, who is now living in Washington with her aunt. Newland's mother invites Sillerton Jackson for dinner with Janey, May, and Archer, and, as always, they gossip. Jackson feels Regina's family is going to be dishonored, as New York society does not tolerate shady business dealings. The gossip changes once again to Ellen: Mrs. Archer, May, and the family are not happy with her refusal to go back to her husband. Later, in the library, Jackson indicates to Newland that Lefferts and many others believe Ellen has taken money from Beaufort because her family reduced her allowance. Once again, Newland is unaware of the allowance reduction, and he is very angry at the implications of a financial relationship between Ellen and Beaufort. Driving home with May, Newland notices that she is unusually silent and he knows she is thinking about Ellen. Before retiring, he tells May that he will be going to Washington on business. May knows he is going to see Ellen, and she sends him a clear signal that she knows and that the family is displeased by his recent actions and opinions. When he complains about a smoky lamp, she says that the problem is solved if one blows the lamp out.

# Commentary

Wharton finally reveals a pattern that has been developing behind the scenes since Newland bought the yellow roses for Ellen and mentioned it to May. May's sense of self-confidence at Newport, her comments about Ellen being happier back in Europe with her husband, and the new Olenski proposals unknown to Newland set the stage for the family closing ranks. Ellen is expensive to support and, though she is informed about what is socially expected, she chooses not to follow custom. She simply is different, a Bohemian who keeps artistic companions. She will obviously be one of those "sacrifices" that must be made to keep the social patterns intact. Because Newland is attracted to her, he is to be kept outside the family decisions.

**Theme**

These chapters make Wharton's theories of change in society very clear. Alterations happen very slowly, often appearing as small cracks that later spread. Newland says, "New York managed its transitions: conspiring to ignore them till they were well over, and then, in all good faith, imagine that they had taken place in the preceding age." The family spokeswoman, Mrs. Archer, sees only small changes each year and denounces them soundly, but all the while we see new "acceptable" people (like Mrs. Struthers), new buildings, new machines, and new ideas (such as wearing Paris fashions immediately) introduced. It seems that the nouveau riche—like Beaufort—are now setting the fashion trends.

**Theme**

The parallel downfalls of Beaufort with New Yorkers and Ellen with her family are discussed. Men are chastised for illegal financial dealings, but forgiven immoral affairs; women are kept financially dependent and ostracized for immoral affairs. Concern that Regina's family will be dragged down in the dirt with Beaufort's shady financial dealings is one example. At the same time, Ellen's position with the family is tenuous at best. Mrs. Manson Mingott no longer defends Ellen's decisions; Mrs. Welland believes that Ellen has sunk to her own level (which seems to be among artists and Bohemians), and makes a snide remark that she is "a great favorite of the gentlemen."

Even Jackson implies that she has been accepting money from Beaufort. The comments irritate Newland because they highlight his intellectual conflict between conservative values and his desire to believe Ellen is above these standards.

Character Insight

These chapters develop a clear picture of the state of Newland and May's marriage after two years. No doubt remains in Newland's mind that May is her mother's image, with her "firm clear tone" of voice. Throughout this novel the social attitudes of their society have been passed down from mother to daughter and father to son. It is becoming clearer that May has quietly controlled their lives and Newland's access to information about family decisions. In her own deliberate and studied way, she has become Mrs. Welland, who soothes her husband, manages his every mood, and smoothes over the disagreements. Newland makes the following realization about his wife: "How young she is! For what endless years this life will have to go on!"

Literary Device

Throughout the novel Wharton has described the nonverbal messages that New York society—as well as husbands and wives—uses in the 1870s. Those who know the code understand the messages. Clearly, in this chapter, Wharton breaks her silence and decodes May's message for Newland. She knows that he is going to see Ellen. Furthermore, she does not understand why he defies the entire family—as well as common sense—in encouraging Ellen not to return to her husband. She hopes he will consider the consequences of that advice. That she tells him this with her "bright housekeeping air" and looks him straight in the eye only exasperates him. May is firm in her own legal and ethical position in his life. She knows he will come back to her because the social patterns and legal ties are too deeply ingrained in him. Allowing him to see Ellen is the equivalent of blowing an irksome candle out. Like her mother, she realizes this too shall pass.

# Book 2
# Chapters XXVII–XXX

## Summary

The following Wednesday, Newland's plans to go to Washington are postponed by a crisis in Beaufort's business affairs. Scandal has caused a run on the bank and Julius Beaufort is anathema. Much talk is heard about "poor Regina" and how "her duty is at his side." In the midst of all this, Newland receives a message from May to come to old Catherine Mingott's because Catherine has had a slight stroke.

Upon arriving he discovers that Regina Beaufort visited Mrs. Mingott the night before, appealing to her to stand by the Beauforts with family loyalty. Humorously, Newland's father-in-law is in bed and will probably stay there, allowing the ladies to handle this problem. Newland listens to the family discussion and agrees with them that "in the old days," husband and wife shared the same disgrace. Mrs. Mingott has requested Ellen's presence and Newland must arrange a telegram. May and her mother hastily agree that it is too bad Newland's and Ellen's trains will probably pass each other. As Newland leaves, he hears May pointedly exclaim that Granny probably wants to convince Ellen to rejoin her husband, the Count.

The next day Catherine is slightly better and decides she will announce her stroke as indigestion. The Countess's reply announces that she will be arriving the next day by train in Jersey City. Newland suggests he meet her train and Mrs. Welland agrees. May finds it odd that Newland can do this when he has led her to believe he must be in Washington for a patent case. He says it has been postponed and she finds that odd also because Newland's boss is going to Washington on a huge patent case. May's insistence on catching Newland in his lie is very uncharacteristic of May. They both know he is lying. But, forgetting this, he thinks of the luxurious two hours he will have with Ellen on the carriage ride back.

As Newland he waits for Ellen's train, he thinks about the predictions of experts about a future where there will be no need for a ferry because a tunnel will take trains under the Hudson. There will be ships that will cross the Atlantic in five days, flying machines, electrical lights, and communication without telegraph wires.

In his mind Newland concocts a romantic dream of what he wants to say while he and Ellen ride together. When she arrives, he unbuttons her glove and kisses the palm of her hand. She pulls away. Forgetting all he meant to say, he tells her of M. Riviere's visit and asks if he helped her leave her husband. When she says "yes" a remarkable conversation follows with Newland dreaming dreams that cannot come true and the Countess speaking with frank realism. He says that their "being together and not together" cannot last. Suddenly, Ellen says he should not have come, and kisses him on the lips, showing her love for him. In considering their options, he suggests that she could be his mistress and run away with him. Ellen invalidates the option, asking what country they will run to where they can live in honor. She implies that she has had an affair and says, "I know what it looks like there." Seeing no way to have the woman he loves, Newland painfully leaves the carriage in the falling snow and walks home. The carriage rolls away and he realizes his tears have frozen to his eyelashes.

That evening the air is stifling in the Archer household. Newland notices that May looks tired and pale. They are dining in and he lies once again about why he left the carriage ride early. May does not refer to Ellen once during dinner, an "ominous sign." Afterward they go to the library. As he considers the rest of his life with this unimaginative wife who is fast becoming her mother, he feels closed in and opens the library window to the icy night. When May protests, saying that he will catch his death of cold, he thinks that he has already been dead for months. Guiltily, he conjectures how his life would be different if May would die young and set him free. She has no clue that he is unhappy and when he declares that he should never be happy unless he can open windows, the thought goes right over her unimaginative head. This is the moment when he realizes he can never have Ellen and he will be May's husband forever.

Six or seven days pass and May suggests that Archer go alone to Granny Mingott's home. He is hoping he will see Ellen and be able to ask her the date of her departure for Washington. He goes to Mrs. Mingott's and during their conversation Catherine makes a strange statement when she says it is a pity that Ellen did not marry him. He discovers from Catherine what the family has not told him. The Count's proposals were very lucrative and the family wanted Catherine to cut Ellen's allowance so that she would be forced to return to her husband.

But Catherine says she will not allow Ellen to be shut in a cage again. Instead, Ellen will stay and nurse her. Newland interprets this to mean that Ellen wants to be close to him. Mrs. Mingott asks Newland to announce her decision to the family and defend it. Meanwhile, Ellen has gone to see Regina Beaufort and Catherine believes them both to be courageous women. She tells Newland to give her love to May but not tell her about their conversation.

## Commentary

**Theme**

Husbands and wives, scandals and lies. These chapters are quickly bringing the novel to its conclusion by highlighting the morality of the 1870s and the dilemmas it creates. First is the problem of the Beauforts: Family loyalty versus dishonor is the conflict that must be resolved. "The whole of New York was darkened by the tale of Beaufort's dishonour." After Regina's visit to old Mrs. Mingott and her subsequent stroke, little sympathy exists for Regina's role. The polite and correct thing would be to retire to North Carolina where they have a racing stable and Julius can be a "horse dealer" in truth. Newland and May's opinion is the same: in sickness, health, and scandal, the husband and wife share equally. Ellen, however, sympathizes with Regina saying, "She's the wife of a scoundrel . . . and so am I, and yet all my family wants me to go back to him." When others will not visit the fallen Regina, Ellen will.

**Character Insight**

Second, Newland is caught in a web of lies. May's insistence that he explain himself over the change in litigation and trip to Washington, reveals that she knows he is lying. Her sadness at his actions reveals a major theme of Wharton's novel: They are products of the culture and code in which they live. Honor demands they stay husband and wife, and even if May cannot discuss his love for Ellen aloud, she certainly is aware of his unhappiness and her failure to keep his affection.

Ellen is the realist in this entire situation. She realizes that the societal principles and habits are what they would lose if they stooped to an affair. Newland made her see this when he defended her right to leave her husband and live a lonely life, but an honorable one. A clandestine affair would mean an end to the principles decent people hold to be true. He is the romantic, wanting to have Ellen near him, but not considering the price she would pay in her loneliness. He romantically says, "Each time you happen to me all over again."

**Literary Device**

When Ellen kisses Archer and he realizes how much she loves him, he envisions a life where he can be married to May but have Ellen too. A product of his time, male gratification is the driving force behind his decision. When she says the word "mistress," he thinks it crude, coming from a woman. He is not a man to break social conventions, while she looks at life more realistically. He exclaims, "I want somehow to get away with you into a world where words like that—categories like that—won't exist . . . ." The realist, Ellen, knows that even if they ran away together, their love would become a shabby parody of life where they would end up in a smaller, dingier world. She asks, "Oh, my dear—where is that country? Have you ever been there?" She has lived outside the world of genteel New Yorkers and she knows Newland is inherently bound to that life and would be unhappy and not himself without it.

When he is with May in the privacy of their library, all of Newland's longing is revealed when he looks at her head bent over her embroidery and realizes this is the life he will have to live. Ellen is right: They cannot hurt those to whom they are bound. He will live a death in life, bound to this unimaginative woman forever.

## Glossary

**probity**   uprightness in one's dealings; integrity.

**litigants**   parties to a lawsuit.

**valetudinarian**   one who thinks constantly and anxiously about one's own health.

**Gorgon**   in Greek mythology, any of three sisters with snakes for hair, so horrible that the beholder is turned to stone.

**Spartan**   like or characteristic of the Spartans, who were famous for being warlike, brave, stoical, severe, frugal, and highly disciplined.

# Book 2
# Chapters XXXI–XXXIII

## Summary

Newland's plan is to speak to Ellen, find out what train she will take to Washington, join her, and run away with her to Japan. He will leave a note for May. However, he drops this plan with relief when he learns from Mrs. Mingott that Ellen will be staying with her.

On his walk home, he sees Ellen leaving the Beaufort house and stops to speak with her. Unfortunately, Lawrence Lefferts and young Chivers are passing and see them. Newland winces at their discovery and wonders how he and Ellen can live such a covert existence. He pleads with Ellen to meet him alone at the Metropolitan Museum the next day, but she appears to dislike this idea. Despite his earlier theoretical championship of Ellen's freedom as a single woman, his next words indicate his real feelings because after she leaves he says, almost contemptuously, "she'll come!"

The following day, they meet at the museum amidst the wreckage of earlier civilizations. Discussing their future, she explains that her stay with her grandmother is to keep them from "doing irreparable harm" to those who love them. However, she reluctantly gives in to Newland's pressure; she agrees to a future brief sexual encounter, after which she is determined go back to Europe. He feels this intimacy will give him the power to pressure her into staying. Then Newland goes home to May who greets him with the news that she saw Ellen at Mrs. Mingott's and they had "a really good talk." She feels she has misjudged Ellen. The following evening, the van der Luydens attend a small dinner at Mrs. Archer's home before going to the opera. Sillerton Jackson, Newland, and May are also there. They discuss Ellen at some length and disapprove of her taking Mrs. Mingott's carriage to the Beaufort's house. After dinner they attend the opera and Newland recalls that it was the same opera they saw the night he met Ellen. May is wearing her made-over wedding dress and she looks the same after two years except for her paleness. He remembers her saying that she could not have her happiness made out of a wrong to someone else. Deciding to confess all and ask for his freedom, Newland pleads a headache and they go home.

At home they settle into the library, but before he can confess, May reveals that Mrs. Manson Mingott has given Ellen an allowance and she is going back to Europe. May had received a letter from Ellen that very afternoon saying that it would be useless for her friends to urge her to change her mind. Cryptically, May adds, "I think she understands everything," and goes to bed. Newland is dumbfounded.

Newland later meets with Mrs. Mingott and when he returns home that evening, May announces a going-away dinner for Ellen. She is very assertive when Newland questions her reasons, and she explains that her mother agrees it is the thing to do. The farewell dinner will be their first big dinner since their marriage. It has been 10 days since Newland saw Ellen and he muses that she will return to Europe and he will follow.

The night of the dinner arrives and when all are assembled Ellen appears, pale and "lusterless." Every glance at her reminds Newland of memories of his love. Now that Ellen is leaving, the Mingotts and Wellands express their affection for her; it is obvious to Newland that this is "a tribal rally around a kinswoman about to be eliminated from the tribe." Suddenly, Newland realizes that the entire family believes he and Ellen are lovers and they are separating them in the most civilized manner possible. Throughout the evening, Newland and Ellen exchange pleasantries, aware that all eyes are on them.

The gentlemen retire to their cigars. Lefferts expounds on the decline of values in New York society, and eventually the men return to the drawing room and "May's triumphant eyes." Newland realizes she shares the belief that he and Ellen are lovers. May kisses Ellen's cheek, vanquishing the foe, and Newland accompanies Ellen to the hall, putting her cloak on her shoulders. When he thinks they might be alone for a moment, the van der Luydens appear and announce they are driving Ellen. He tells her that he will see her soon in Paris, and she correctly says it would be nice if he and May could come. Then she is gone.

The dinner is over and Newland and May are in the library. Newland starts to confess once again, but says instead that he needs to go on a long trip because he is very tired. May explains that the doctor might not let her go along, and she reveals that she has already told both her mother and mother-in-law that she is pregnant. It dawns on Newland that the conversation she had with Ellen two weeks earlier was about her pregnancy. She watches Newland intently as she asks if he minds. In questioning her, he finds that she told Ellen this news long before she was sure.

# Commentary

**Character Insight**

Wharton shows the reader that Newland cannot justify going against all the ethical foundations of his society. Wanting to believe he is different from men who conduct surreptitious affairs, Newland spends considerable time rationalizing his conduct. It was fine for Mrs. Thorley Rushworth to have an affair because women were not expected to be truthful in matters of love. In fact, women had to be devious because they were powerless. But no one laughed at a lawfully wedded wife who was misled. Men were to keep to a higher standard and were despised if they sowed wild oats after marriage. While he might mouth the words to Sillerton Jackson that women should be "free," he looks on Ellen with contempt when he thinks that he can persuade her to come to him. Wharton further shows his discomfort as he passes his home, and thinks that his wife is within, along with honor and decency and all the comforts of doing the expected thing.

**Literary Device**

Time takes on a symbolic value at the art museum. Newland and Ellen meet amidst objects from former civilizations that are now "time-blurred." Many are marked with the designation "use unknown," and Ellen ironically remarks that these objects once belonged to forgotten people who used and valued them. To Ellen it seems cruel that nothing lasts or matters eventually. These objects bring to mind the various exacting sets of trousseau items and the numerous duties of Newland before his wedding. He commented then on the trifling concern for "form" and felt that those little details of so-called civilized life now seemed like the exercises of medieval scholars who argued over mystical or abstract terminology. Time, with its relentless power, sweeps away the trinkets, items, and fussy social distinctions with a "use unknown" label, showing their meaninglessness. Wharton reaches amazing heights in describing the protective walls of the family surrounding marriage among one's own kind at the farewell dinner. The evening seems genuine, unselfish, and generous, but it is really a calculated and elaborate production by the family and May. They never leave Newland alone with Ellen for a moment. Amidst the gilt-edged menus and multitude of servants, this society sacrifices one of its own to protect the family. Earlier in the book, when Newland was tempted by his feelings for Ellen, the wedding was quickly planned. Now, when Newland is about to confess all, a pregnancy is announced. Like a player in a chess game, May has considered his possible moves and made defensive moves to thwart him, with the support of both mothers. They know Newland would never leave a pregnant wife and go to Europe with Ellen. Newland does not realize it, but he has been outside of the family information channels for some time.

**Theme**

The last chapters also bring to the forefront the powerful social order that approves of May's actions. The van der Luydens had fled to Skuytercliff when the Beaufort scandal erupted. Now they "reluctantly but heroically" return to put the social order right. Newland still does not realize the bargaining and plotting that have been going on behind the scenes in the family. When May announces the farewell dinner, she alludes to a conversation with Ellen when she indicated that she and Newland were one in their sentiments. Later it becomes obvious that May used her pregnancy as leverage with Ellen long before May was sure that she was pregnant.

This whole subterfuge supports Wharton's major theme that the emotions of the individual must be sacrificed for the preservation of those values that make life worth living and keep the social order intact—values that existed in the pre-World War I society of old New York.

**Character Insight**

These final chapters also highlight May and Newland's roles. Wharton paints a change in May that careful readers notice but Newland overlooks. May lays her hand on his shoulder "with one of her rare caresses." Despite May's pallor, Wharton mentions her animated conversation and "unnatural vividness" more than once. May lingers over his words, hugs and kisses him, and seems to be showing him fond attention. This comes on the heels of her comment that she and Ellen had a good talk at Granny Mingott's. Wharton is setting up May's final triumph. Newland's role at this dinner is that of an observer, almost floating over the scene in an after-death experience. He suddenly realizes as he looks at the dining family members that "by means yet unknown to him, the separation between himself and the partner of his guilt had been achieved." It is the civilized way of taking a life without a drop of blood being shed.

## Glossary

**fatuity**   complacent stupidity; smug foolishness.

**Ilium**   the Latin name for Troy, an ancient Phrygian city in northwest Asia Minor.

**sarcophagi**   among the ancient Greeks, Romans, and Egyptians, limestone coffins or tombs, often inscribed and elaborately ornamented.

**repast**   food and drink for a meal.

**jardiniere**   an ornamental bowl, pot, or stand for flowers or plants.

**affability**   cordial quality; friendliness or gentleness.

**philippic**   a long, vehement speech, especially one of denunciation; harangue.

**"dressed by Poole"**   Lefferts' clothes are from fashionable Saville Row in London where Henry Poole and Company are tailors to "gentlemen."

# Book 2
# Chapter XXXIV

## Summary

Twenty-six years later in a new century, Newland Archer, age 57, is sitting in his library on East 39th Street, having just returned from a ceremony for new galleries in the Metropolitan Museum. He is in a reflective mood, brought about by his memories of meeting the Countess there years ago. In his library he remembers May announcing her pregnancy; their delicate son, Dallas, being christened and later taking his first steps; their daughter, Mary, becoming engaged to one of Reggie Chivers' dull sons and her radiant face as Newland kissed her here on her wedding day; and his conversations with Theodore Roosevelt, a family friend, who stayed overnight. Roosevelt talked Newland into running for public office, as Ned Winsett had often urged him to do. Spending only one term in the State Assembly, Newland has settled into the role of elder statesman, consulted on projects for the city and become involved in philanthropic work.

His marriage to May was dull but dignified, and he mourns her sincerely; she had died two years before of the infectious pneumonia through which she had nursed their third child, Bill, back to health. Newland looks at May's first picture, still in its place near the inkstand, and muses that she remained unchanged—like her photo—until her death. Even the children hesitated to take away her ingenuous thoughts with their cold, new-century realities. The telephone rings and Newland speaks with Dallas, his architect son who is calling long distance from Chicago. Dallas' voice sounds so close it is amazing, and Newland listens as Dallas asks him to go to Europe with him on a job. Newland's son is to be married on June 5 to Fanny Beaufort, daughter of Julius and Fanny Ring, who married years ago following the death of Regina Beaufort. Times have changed and no one criticizes this union.

Newland accompanies his son to Paris. All those years ago, he told Ellen he would see her in Paris, but he never kept that promise. Although he thought of himself as a dashing and romantic figure then, he now realizes he is a middle-aged relic. Ellen never went back to her husband and never married either. The Count died, leaving her a widow, living in Paris.

Dallas' fiancée, Fanny, asked him to do several things, one of which was to see the Countess Olenska who had befriended her when she was in school in Europe. So Dallas tells his father he has accepted an invitation for them to call on the countess. He reveals to Newland that he knows the countess was once "your Fanny." Shocked, Newland asks him why he thinks that. Dallas simply states that his dying mother told him that Newland had "given up the thing [he] most wanted" and revealed her knowledge of his love for the countess. Newland is stunned to realize that his dutiful and unimaginative wife had known all along, and he is touched that she pitied him for his sacrifice.

Dallas leaves to visit Versailles and Newland roams Paris, thinking of the amazing life Ellen must have had there with museums, art galleries, glittering acquaintances, and a freer world than New York City. He visits the Louvre because she probably haunted that art gallery and he thinks of himself at age 57; the sweet love of springtime is no longer possible, but perhaps they could have the mature companionship of autumn. Later that day, Newland and Dallas walk to the Invalides and pause outside Ellen's apartment. The day is fading and the view is peaceful and pleasant. Newland sits down on a bench and convinces Dallas to go up to Ellen's apartment without him, as he wants to sit a few minutes and collect his thoughts. Dallas is more like the young Newland that Ellen will remember from thirty years ago. After his son leaves, Newland imagines what that meeting will be like and realizes, "It's more real to me here than if I went up." The sun slowly goes down and he stands up and walks back to his hotel.

# Commentary

**Theme**

Chapter 34 is especially important because it brings Wharton's story full circle and reveals the results of decisions made and promises kept. The new century is a world where both lifestyles and social values have changed considerably and Wharton knows that soon World War I will alter everything forever. She looks back on the values of her childhood New York with mixed feelings. She sees the van der Luydens' world as a place where sacrifice was necessary to promulgate the social order, but she also sees the new century where individuals have more freedom as represented by Newland and May's children.

**Literary Device**

Everything about the new century is scientific and technological. The old Metropolitan Museum is now cataloguing items in a "scientific" way. Newland clings to his Eastlake desk despite Dallas' addition of electric lamps and more "modern" furniture. Traditional, colonial architecture is no longer a sign of status and wealth; it has made way for English mezzotints and Chippendale cabinets. Telephones connect people across continents and electricity lights even the night. A voyage across the Atlantic now takes only five days, and there are new-fangled hotels, motor cars, and aeroplanes. Everywhere modern products are changing the lifestyles of Americans, but these products are part of the mass-produced modern world with no deeper meaning. In many ways Wharton reveals that twentieth-century lifestyles are filled with superficial products at the expense of lives with deeper sensitivities and reserves.

Even the social attitudes are changing. May would not recognize this world, nor would she feel comfortable in it. Some things are the same, like Mary's wedding at Grace Church. However, men are now able, like Dallas, to turn interests into occupations. While he inherited his father's love of art, he changed it into architecture where he could use it in a socially acceptable way. Law is no longer the only male job choice. Even Mary is not like her mother in some ways. While she has some of May's traditional values, she is a new woman in that she is more athletic and more tolerant in many areas of her life. Where May could shoot arrows, Mary can climb mountains.

**Literary Device**

Dallas also represents the new generation. His class and age group is more sure, confident, and free. Newland mentions his "assured step and delightful smile," useful to seal contracts with rich, new millionaires. Dallas sees Newland and May's sacrifice as prehistoric. While Newland has tried to teach his son to be more reserved, Dallas revels in a world where husbands and wives can tell each other what they think. His marriage to Fanny Beaufort, sanctioned by Janey's gift of their mother's jewelry, is a symbol of the new society's ability to find a place for those ostracized in the old order. No one remembers the Beaufort scandal anymore, and what was not acceptable in Newland's close and structured world is now permissible.

**Theme**

Wharton brings home, with May's deathbed confession, the idea that the lives of the old wealthy in 1870s New York were totally shaped and conditioned by a context no longer as strong in the new century. Where Newland felt that leaving May for Ellen would mean the loss of "habit, and honour, and all the old decencies," Dallas finds that sacrifice prehistoric. May understood that Newland could have lived no other way. The announcement of her pregnancy sealed forever his choice to leave because he was powerfully locked into a world where that would have been unthinkable. In Newland's young world, May would never have asked him to make such a sacrifice because it was understood that he would. The passions of individuals were surrendered to perpetuate the social order. Now, after World War I, Wharton looks back on that idea with mixed emotions. The New York of the 1870s did not have the social upheaval brought about by the war in Europe, and its traditional outlook from father to son, and mother to daughter, provided a stability that could be treasured, despite its cost to the individual.

In many ways, this last chapter is about the passing of the torch from one generation to another amidst a realization that the old world is over. The day Newland and Ellen met at the museum among the crumbling relics and uncertain antiquities, he realized that time took away identities, cares, and concerns. Then it was just an abstract idea; now, in twentieth-century Paris, it is a reality. Children are born, christened, grow up, and leave, and parents settle into new roles and eventually die. The photo of Newland's young wife, May, is frozen in time, just as his image of Ellen will remain forever in the 1870s. Seeing himself as a "grey relic of a man," Newland realizes that he holds fast to habit and prefers the world of his youth. The new world belongs to his son and those like him, less sensitive than their parents, but infinitely more free to follow their passions. Deciding to remember the exotic Ellen as a memory from his past and a symbol of his freedom from social restraints, Newland walks into the dusk in the lingering last words of the novel. Wharton suggests that only his memories of their love in that earlier time have any meaning. That love belonged to a different, more ordered time and if left alone, its memory can be cherished.

# Glossary

**confabulations**   informal conversations; chats.

**mezzotints**   engravings or prints produced on copper or steel plates by scraping or polishing parts of roughened surfaces to produce impressions of light and shade.

**Mauretania**   a fashionable British Cunard Line ship which made its maiden voyage in 1907. A sister to the *Lusitania* which was torpedoed during World War I, the Mauretania was known for its fast ocean crossings. Here, Dallas suggests he and Newland take the *Mauretania*.

**proclivities**   natural or habitual tendencies or inclinations, especially toward something discreditable.

**trenchant**   keen; penetrating; incisive.

**ethereally**   in a way that is not of the earth; heavenly.

# CHARACTER ANALYSES

# Newland Archer

Newland Archer is a study in intellectual conflict, but under the surface little contradiction actually exists, as his wife knows well. He first appears at the opera, where he is so steeped in the social graces that even his hair is carefully parted by "two silver-backed brushes with his monogram in blue enamel," and he never appears in public without a flower in his buttonhole. He contemplates his perfect wife, May, and seems quite at ease as her parents buy his house and even the brougham he drives. So correct is he that when he impulsively sends yellow roses to Ellen, he is conscience stricken and must tell his future wife. Even his meticulous attention to the list of his duties before his own wedding is typical of Newland's conformity. In a key scene when he fails to call to Ellen at the Newport shore, he once again shows that actually doing the unconventional is beyond the bounds of possibility for him. Countess Ellen Olenska represents a dream of the unconventional, more passionate life for which he will never sacrifice everything. He sometimes feels he is being smothered in his social position, but he will only dream about a life outside the tight parameters of his class and duty. May uses her knowledge of his commitment to the social values of his class to keep him faithful. Even 26 years after his wedding, he realizes that his conventional life has the comforting feeling of the place where he belongs. He is a relic in the twentieth century, where increased personal freedom is changing life forever. The sexual double standard for men and women is an intellectual battleground in his mind. In several scenes, he debates whether this standard is valid, especially when he meets and desires Ellen. In the long run, however, he overlooks Lefferts' affairs because it is the way of his world. He talks convincingly about honor and integrity, but selfishly he wants both his wife and Ellen, and briefly he contemplates a hole-in-the-corner affair, not caring on an emotional level about the price Ellen will pay.

Newland also longs for a life of passion, intellectual stimulation, and freedom, represented by both Ellen Olenska and Ned Winsett. He is unfulfilled by his "gentlemanly pursuit" of law and feels that he wants the sophisticated and passionate Ellen. But in the end he remains true to his station in life and that four-letter word, "duty." Wharton uses his character to show the ironies of 1870s society as well as the extremes in social thought represented by his relationships with Countess Ellen Olenska and May Welland Archer.

# May Welland Archer

A perfect product of the social code, May Welland Archer begins the novel in ignorance and ends it in wisdom. When she first appears, she is the personification of innocence. She marries Newland and her slim intellectual abilities never vary, but her wisdom in manipulating Newland grows immensely. Wharton exercises considerable talent in showing May through the eyes of Newland Archer, whose vision of her is frozen in time like her photograph on his desk. He sees too late that she outmaneuvers him at every turn and that she knows of his unhappiness.

She is her mother's daughter. In Florida, her mother voices narrow and snobbish attitudes that later parallel May's own comments about people she meets on her honeymoon. Always worrying about what her mother will think, May manages Newland's life; she arranges every minute of his schedule at Newport, becoming the image of her mother after two years of marriage. Newland is kept on a short leash and it is a wonder that he is able to get away to meet Ellen.

Her strategic actions throughout the novel show that she has learned well at her mother's side. She sends Newland a letter from Florida reminding him of her kindness just as he is ready to fall for Ellen's charms. Her telegram in Chapter 18 anticipates his temptation and closes the door on it. She is firm about her position as his wife, and she uses the ruse of pregnancy to finally vanquish Ellen forever. In a society where women have little power, they use what they can. Her suggestion that they give a "last dinner" for Ellen shows how she has grown in wisdom and the determination to hold on to what she has. She knows her husband, and even her deathbed confession to Dallas demonstrates her knowledge of Newland's unhappiness but her total understanding of duty and their shared values.

She cannot fulfill Newland's desires for an emotional life or intellectual stimulation, but with true Wharton irony she does symbolize the perfect wife and marriage partner for his social class and time. Like other women, she keeps Newland on the straight and narrow, pronouncing any deviation from the norm to be "vulgar" and unthinkable. May Welland is exactly what she has been trained to be: the perfect helpmate of civilized society in wealthy 1870s New York.

# Countess Ellen Olenska

Ellen, the Countess Olenska, fulfills Newland's longing for an emotional fantasy life. Her words, her unconventional taste in clothing and interior decorating, and her attitudes symbolize the exotic to traditional Newland. She causes him to question his narrow existence and brings out his protective instincts. Where May is ice, Ellen is fire. Ellen's élan and style would be at home in Europe, but seem unduly passionate and unorthodox in New York City.

Emotionally, she is the opposite of May Welland Archer. She shows compassion to Regina Beaufort, a fellow victim of social censure. Often she causes Newland to question why everyone must be and act exactly alike. Her tolerance for the mavericks of society reveals her benevolence, a trait unappreciated by New Yorkers. This makes it possible for May to use Ellen's softness to her advantage because she knows that Ellen will never run away with Newland when May reveals her possible pregnancy. Ellen's lack of concern for social rules and etiquette make her a target of malicious tongues, but a heroine of the dispossessed. Unlike the inane society wives, she has a mind of her own and uses it well and with concern for others. Unfortunately, this seals her fate because New York society has a difficult time understanding single women living apart from their husbands, and her lifestyle makes her family, as well as their social class, nervous.

Ellen falls in love with Newland, but she is a realist. She asks him, "Does no one want to know the truth here?" as she notices the narrow hypocrisy of his social world. Ellen knows that they cannot live a life outside of convention without hurting others. She reminds Newland that social, religious, and class standards must be upheld. A clandestine affair with him means no honor, no principles, and no happiness. As she explains, "I can't love you unless I give you up." Unselfish in doing exactly that, she realizes they are "chained to their destinies" and she leaves because an unconventional life cannot survive in 1870s New York.

The story of her life after her departure is revealed secondhand. The reader is left to consider that she never married again and she lived a single woman's life in Paris. She was presumably able to savor the life of art museums, parties long into the night, possible lovers, wine, and exquisite food. This broader, more passionate life would not have been hers in New York. She remains a mystery to Newland to the end, but a symbol of his imagined life of the soul.

# Mrs. Manson Mingott

The former Catherine Spicer of Staten Island and widow of Manson Mingott is Ellen's grandmother. What is most memorable about her is her immense size. Despite her lively eyes and interesting conversation, she lives in an obese body. A widow at 28, she had single-mindedly used her will and ambition to win and maintain a social position, and her attention to values of decency in her private life had won society's approval. She hobnobbed with the fashionable and the corrupt of European society, and she knew intimate friends and admirers on both continents.

Her love for her granddaughter, Ellen, is never in question. She, like Ellen, is a realist and in "cold-blooded complacency" declares that Ellen's life is over after she leaves the Count. Mrs. Mingott sees clearly that Ellen's future is either an unhappy affair with Newland or an unhappy marriage with the Count, and of the two possibilities, the second is more socially acceptable. Catherine knows from vast experience that "socially acceptable," while not always bringing happiness, is far more fulfilling than living on the outskirts of polite society.

She survives the storms of Ellen's decisions and undisputed lack of social etiquette, and she champions Ellen's cause with the family. A realist, she turns to Newland when matters of finance and divorce must be settled. But when Regina Beaufort asks for her backing as the family matriarch over Julius Beaufort's scandalous behavior, it is too much for the old lady. The realist ever, she makes it financially possible for Ellen to live on her own, single, but in charge of her destiny.

# CRITICAL ESSAY

**Themes in *The Age of Innocence***

For another critical essay, visit www.cliffs.com/
extras.

# Themes in *The Age of Innocence*

By the time Edith Wharton wrote *The Age of Innocence,* she had seen World War I destroy much of the world as she knew it. She looked back on her early years in New York as a time of social continuity, and felt that the passing of values from parent to child had a civilizing influence. However, she also saw the hypocrisy and cruelty practiced by individuals who wore the veneer of respectability. Both of these ideas are seen throughout *The Age of Innocence,* making it a timeless novel of both the Gilded Age and of social change.

## Values

Wharton was often critical of the rigidity of the social code, but she saw its purpose of handing down values and replicating culture. Order, loyalty, tradition, and duty are all values upheld and also criticized in her novel. Order is epitomized by the repetition of certain rituals. Newland Archer's wife must be sexually innocent and pretend not to know about affairs or passions. When we first meet May Welland we see her in white with white lilies of the valley, oblivious to the sexual innuendoes of the play she is watching. Later, the reader discovers that she knew all along of Newland's passion for Ellen, but she followed the accepted code of ignorance. Order is maintained by these understood practices. The wedding at Grace Church is a perfect replication of the order in which things must be done; even Newland has a list of socially mandated duties to perform. This is the way civilization continues.

Loyalty is also a virtue, not only among families and marriages, but also among men. Newland must go to the Mingott box to show his family loyalty when the notorious Ellen arrives. Ellen's "last supper" is presided over by the family showing its loyalty to May and ousting the interloper. At that same dinner, Lawrence Lefferts asks Newland to "cover" for him and lie to give him an alibi so that he can carry on an affair. Newland will lie and tell no one. Loyalty must be maintained.

Tradition also is a way of passing on values. The ritual of the wedding calls, the annual Beaufort ball, the season, the gowns that are bought but put away for two years, and the details of Newland's wedding are all examples of attitudes or events that are handed down from parent to child. This maintains desired order.

Duty is the idea that one soldiers on with a smile even in the face of adversity. Newland's commitment to May after she tells him she is pregnant is a duty understood. His acceptance that he will stay with her in a boring marriage even in the face of frustration is, in the end, what makes civilization work. At every turn of his passion, Newland sees the door closed by May and duty.

## Enforcing the Code

Wharton's New York society rigidly enforces the social code. Until the van der Luydens come to her rescue, society refuses to welcome Ellen because she is a woman who has left her husband. If, however, the van der Luydens extend a dinner invitation to socially accept Ellen, then New Yorkers have a clear signal of what is expected. Mrs. Archer clearly explains this understood social code when she says that men are expected to have affairs as in "boys will be boys," but women are expected to be faithful to the end. If a person considers breaking the code, the eyes of society are everywhere. When Newland is out for a walk and sees Ellen, he worries about the eyes of Lefferts and Chivers who happen to see them. Because Newland has been in on many of the cigar-smoking gatherings of his fellow men, he knows the judgments that will arise about his meeting with Ellen. Despite that knowledge, Newland does not realize that the family has been plotting behind his back to keep him faithful. Ignoring the code does not work: This is evident because Ellen (having lived in a more open society) pays a price, even among her family, for doing so.

## Personal Freedom

Because the social code enforces such rules as are good for society, personal freedom is sacrificed. Newland cannot follow his passion; he must do his duty. Ellen realizes that they cannot have an affair—no matter how much they might love each other—and maintain social integrity. To be married to a despicable husband who has numerous affairs and treats his wife badly is condoned by the social code, to divorce that husband is not.

## Hypocrisy

Loopholes can be found in this code and those who find them might often be despised, but they are still tolerated in this society. Lawrence Lefferts is the prime example of hypocrisy, having numerous affairs but extolling Christian virtues and snubbing Ellen for leaving her husband.

Newland realizes that if he leaves May for Ellen, society's sympathy will be with May, even though he could have a quiet affair and get away with it. May must pretend that she does not know Newland is in love with her cousin, but from her deathbed confession the reader sees that she lived with this knowledge most of her life. In the age of alleged innocence, hypocrisy abounds.

## Appearances and Reality

True to the Gilded Age, Wharton's society knows that appearance is everything. Ellen realizes the hypocrisy of New Yorkers from her first glimpse of them. She tells Newland on many occasions that they do not want to hear the truth; they would rather pretend. May gives a lavish going-away dinner for Ellen. It is a huge success, but under the surface it is a "civilized" triumph because of May's position as "wife." Similarly, all of New York turns out for the annual Beaufort Ball, but under the surface they know he is scandalous and uncomfortably not one of theirs. His adultery and that of Lefferts are acceptable as long as they are discreet.

## Men and Women

In Wharton's world, women are sexually innocent, not expected to have affairs, acknowledge those of their husbands, or ever divorce. The only power they have is the power that May uses: duty, loyalty, and (most of all) pregnancy. Victorian women are beautiful trophies but innocent brides. Single, they are ornaments like May with her exciting and radiant glow, and married, they are mothers who keep the home and provide continuity. Ellen's sin is that she refuses to accept these restrictions and will not lie about loving Newland. Men too have restrictions, one of which is their jobs. The only acceptable vocation for Newland is the law, however boring. He must not dirty his hands in business or "trade."

# CliffsNotes Review

Use this "CliffsNotes Review" to test your understanding of the original text and reinforce what you have learned in this book. After you work through the "Q&A," "Essay Questions," "Identify the Quote," and (fun and useful) "Practice Projects" sections, you are well on your way to understanding a comprehensive and meaningful interpretation of *The Age of Innocence.*

## Q&A

**1.** The stage—both opera and theatre—mirrors the novel's plot. The two examples of stage productions used by Wharton are

   **a.** *The Tempest* and *Aida*

   **b.** *Faust* and *The Shaughraun*

   **c.** *Othello* and *The Marriage of Figaro*

   **d.** *The Magic Flute* and *Awake and Sing*

**2.** When Newland is tempted by his feelings for Ellen, he pursues May to

   **a.** London

   **b.** San Francisco

   **c.** Boston

   **d.** Florida

**3.** When Newland and Ellen meet secretly to discuss their future, the location is

   **a.** The Academy of Music

   **b.** The Metropolitan Museum

   **c.** Washington Square

   **d.** Wallack's Theatre

**4.** Ned Winsett is a minor character but is used

   **a.** To demonstrate the drawbacks of the artistic life

   **b.** To show the advantages of the leisure-class life

   **c.** As a symbol of the New Rich

   **d.** As an example of one of May's friends

**5.** May dies

    **a.** In a carriage accident

    **b.** In childbirth

    **c.** Of pneumonia

    **d.** In her sleep of a stroke

**Answers:** (1) b. (2) d. (3) b. (4) a. (5) c.

# Identify the Quote

Identify the speaker and listener in the following significant quotations from the novel:

**1.** "I want—I want somehow to get away with you into a world where words like that—categories like that—won't exist. Where we shall be simply two human beings who love each other, who are the whole of life to each other, and nothing else on earth will matter."

**2.** "But I'm afraid you can't, dear . . . . Not unless you'll take me with you...That is, if the doctors will let me go . . . but I'm afraid they won't. For you see . . . I've been sure since this morning of something I've been so longing and hoping for."

**3.** "Wasn't she—once—your Fanny?"

**4.** "At least it was you who made me understand that under the dullness there are things so fine and sensitive and delicate that even those I most cared for in my other life look cheap in comparison."

**5.** "The van der Luydens show it to so few people. But they opened it for Ellen, it seems, and she told me what a darling place it was: she says it's the only house she's seen in America that she could imagine being perfectly happy in."

**Answers:** (1) Newland, to Ellen in the carriage ride from Penn Station. (2) May, telling Newland she is pregnant. (3) Dallas, speaking to his father in Paris. (4) Ellen, to Newland at their secret lunch on Point Arley. (5) May, speaking to Newland of the Patroon's House.

# Essay Questions

**1.** Discuss Newland, Ellen, and May's characters in terms of your own judgements. How do you evaluate their actions, words, and motivations?

**2.** Wharton often uses surroundings—architecture, paintings, and interior design—to help describe the owner. Choose a person in the novel and use that person's possessions to describe their character.

**3.** One of the major conflicts of the novel is stability versus change. Where does Wharton use that?

**4.** Was Wharton being critical of 1870s America, or was she admiring it? Use evidence to support your view.

**5.** Justify the ending of the novel, staying consistent with Wharton's purposes, themes, and characters.

# Practice Projects

**1.** Research the interior decoration of the period and use illustrations to show several of the items used by Wharton in her interiors.

**2.** Research Edith Wharton's war years and report on her many actions to help others.

**3.** In what ways did Wharton's life influence her novel? Pair up with another person and present an interview with the author.

**4.** Create a Web site for *The Age of Innocence* with principle areas including the author's background, as well as setting, characters, symbols, and themes.

**5.** Act out a key scene in the story and convey the importance of its nature in the context of the book.

**6.** Create a collage that shows the relationships of the characters in the story and explain your thinking to your audience.

**7.** Create an exhibit of photographs from the late 1800s and use quotations from the novel for captions.

# CliffsNotes Resource Center

The learning doesn't need to stop here. CliffsNotes Resource Center shows you the best of the best—links to the best information in print and online about the author and related works. And don't think that this book all we've prepared for you; we've put all kinds of pertinent information at www.cliffs.com. Look for the terrific resources at your favorite bookstore or local library and on the Internet. When you're online, make your first stop www.cliffs.com, where you'll find more incredibly useful information about *The Age of Innocence*.

## Books

This CliffsNotes book provides a meaningful interpretation of *The Age of Innocence*. If you are looking for information about the author and related works, check out these other publications:

*A Backward Glance,* by Edith Wharton, is her autobiography. It discusses her enjoyment of reading, her childhood lack of confidence, her views as a young writer, and her travels and friendships. New York: Appleton-Century, 1934.

*Displaying Women: Spectacles of Leisure in Edith Wharton's New York,* by Maureen E. Montgomery, contains six chapters about the society of old New York. The social calendar, rituals, etiquette, interior decoration, and the role of women are discussed. Bibliography and index. New York: Routledge, 1998.

*The Age of Innocence: A Novel of Ironic Nostalgia,* edited by Linda Wagner-Martin, gives an overall study of the novel, including its historical context, genre, literary themes, and symbols. Part of the Twayne Masterwork Studies. New York; Twayne Publishers, 1996.

*Edith Wharton A to Z: The Essential Guide to the Life and Work,* by Sarah Bird Wright, has literally hundreds of entries and descriptions of places, dates, writings, and biographical facts. New York: Facts on File, 1998.

If you're interested in other books published by Wiley Publishing, Inc., check out these Web sites:

- www.cliffs.com
- www.dummies.com
- www.wiley.com

# Magazines and Journals

Magazines and journals are excellent for additional information about *The Age of Innocence* by Edith Wharton. You may want to check out these publications for information about the author and related works.

DAVIS, JOY L. "The Rituals of Dining in Edith Wharton's *The Age of Innocence.*" *The Midwest Quarterly,* Summer 1993: 465–481. An in-depth discussion of how social ritual and etiquette concealed the darker passions of the novel and the conflict between the Old and New Rich.

FRYER, JUDITH "Purity and Power in *The Age of Innocence.*" *American Literary Realism 17,* 1985: 153–168. Discusses the social attitudes revealed in Wharton's novel.

GRENIER, RICHARD "Society and Edith Wharton." *Commentary,* Dec. 1993: 48–55. Discusses similarities and differences between Wharton's novel and the Scorsese film of 1993.

HADLEY, KATHY MILLER "Ironic Structure and Untold Stories in *The Age of Innocence.*" *Studies in the Novel,* Summer 1991: 262. A critique of Wharton's novel, focusing on the ironic ending of the novel.

# Internet

Check out these Web resources for more information about Edith Wharton and *The Age of Innocence*

American Writers: Edith Wharton Video Lesson Plan, `http://www.americanwriters.org/classroom/videolesson/vlp20_wharton.asp` — C-SPAN's companion site for their televised series on American authors. A wealth of information on the Gilded Age, video clips, social classes, and the role of women.

Edith Wharton Page, `http://www.womenwriters.net/domesticgoddess/wharton1.htm` — contains biography, links, bibliography, and literary criticism.

The Edith Wharton Society Page, `http://guweb2.gonzaga.edu/faculty/campbell/wharton/` — a scholarly Web site run by the society. Contains papers, biography, conferences, bibliography, works online, and links to other sites.

The Lit Network, `http://www.online-literature.com/wharton/` — a biography, links to descriptions of her major works, and the works online.

The San Antonio College LitWeb Edith Wharton Page, `http://www.accd.edu/sac/english/bailey/wharton.htm` — lists Wharton's major works, including online texts, books, and links about Wharton.

Next time you're on the Internet, don't forget to drop by `www.cliffs.com`. We created an online Resource Center that you can use today, tomorrow, and beyond.

# Film and Other Recordings

The following films either adapt *The Age of Innocence* or other novels by Edith Wharton that explore *The Age of Innocence*'s themes.

*The Age of Innocence.* Dir. Wesley Ruggles. Perf. Beverly Bryne, Elliott Dexter, Edith Roberts. Warner Brothers, 1924. This is the earliest film version of the novel with a screenplay by Olga Printzlau. 7 reels, silent.

*The Age of Innocence.* Dir. Philip Moeller. Perf. Irene Dunne, John Boles, Julie Haydon. RKO Radio, 1934. This film version contains sound and is 80–90 minutes long.

*The Age of Innocence.* Dir. Martin Scorsese. Perf. Daniel Day-Lewis, Michelle Pfeiffer, Winona Ryder. Columbia Pictures, 1993. The screenplay by Jay Cocks and Martin Scorsese is 138 minutes long. Missing are the detailed interior decoration descriptions and much of the satire. The ending is more ambiguous in evaluating the characters and the last scene shows Newland's images of Ellen as she was 26 years earlier. This film is faithful to the love story and Edith Wharton's attitudes.

# Index